It's NOT about You

Understanding Purpose Through Your Pain

―⊙―

Valerie Hodge Lane

Creator and Founder of Positive Image Consulting Firm

Kingdom Builders Publications LLC

Valerie H. Lane

Copyright © 2018 Valerie H. Lane
Kingdom Builders Publications

All rights reserved. No part of this book may be reproduced or transmitted in any form or by any means without written permission from the author.

Printed in the USA
SOFT COVER ISBN 978-0-692-15662-9
Library of Congress Control Number 2018951614

Authored by Valerie Hodge Lane

Edited by
Veronica McCullough
Lakisha S. Forrester
Wanda Brown, Editor-n-chief of Kingdom Builders Publications

Cover Design
Darryl Lane
LoMar Designs

He, and any other terms that acknowledges God will be capitalized.

DEDICATION

This book is dedicated to anyone experiencing abuse or has survived any form of abuse. This is my story of growing up in a dysfunctional family and being kept in bondage for years. I am sharing with all of you who have wanted to give up at some point. Although you were abused and misused, you are still more than conquerors. Others may have counted you out or said you would never amount to anything. However, I am here to tell you that there is purpose in your pain. God will set you free, not just for yourselves, but for others. You are integral in building His Kingdom on Earth. We must do His Perfect Will and look forward to living eternally in Heaven.

CONTENTS

	Dedication	iii
	Foreword	iv
	Introduction	vii
	A Love Letter	x
	My Prayer	11
1	It's Not About You	12
2	Getting Pass Your Past	16
3	A Decade of Abuse	19
4	Tore Up from the Floor Up (part 1)	24
5	Tore Up from the Floor Up (part 2)	29
6	Identity Thief	35
7	Dysfunctional Families (Part 1)	40
8	Dysfunctional Families (Part 2)	46
9	The Hedge of Protection	51
10	Getting to the Root of the Problem	53
11	Forever the Victim	60
12	No More Drama	62
13	Popularizing Drama	67
14	Procrastination	69

15	Look Within	74
16	Taking off the Mask	78
17	Determination	85
18	Let Go and Let God	88
19	Change (Part 1)	93
20	Change (Part2)	97
21	Do Not Quit	100
22	Understanding Purpose through your Pain	101
23	A Call to Salvation	104
	Conclusion	105
	Acknowledgments	110
	Bible References	112
	More about the Author	116
	About the Positive Image Consulting Firm	118

FOREWORD

As I read this book, I was touched by all of the testimonies that were recorded. It was a testament to the fact that God can and is willing to help us in the midst of adversity. The common theme throughout this book was synonymous with the title. Oftentimes, as we grapple with life and allow our situations to overtake us, it can become easy to forget that God will turn everything around for our good. But, we must trust His plan, no matter how long it takes.

Valerie H. Lane captivated me as a reader. She stressed that any type of dysfunction, whether created in our childhood or in adulthood, can cause stumbling blocks in our present. However, it does not have to impede our future from becoming great. She not only provided testimonies, but she gave strategies to help us overcome our hurts. She reminded me, in her book, that I have purpose, and that it is not about me. It is all about the work of our Father which art is in Heaven.

Lakisha Forrester
Columbia, SC

INTRODUCTION

Just to hear him call my name was enough to make me shiver. Each time I heard his voice, I knew something bad was about to happen. When he would spank me, I was told to take all my clothes off first. The belt would strike my arms, legs, and backside. At the age of 10, it was difficult to clean my room, cook, and wash dishes to his liking. It was so hard to please him. If one dish had even a speck of food left on it or even a water spot, he would become enraged. I lived in fear of him. No matter how hard I tried to do what he wanted me to do and the way he wanted me to do it, there was just no pleasing him.

At times, I would want to run to momma for help. I could not because she was always so mean to me. Instead of grabbing me and picking me up to console me, she would always tell me I could not do anything right and I would never amount to anything. She always seemed to end her verbal assaults by telling me how ugly I was. Total confusion is what I felt. I wondered why my mommy and daddy didn't love me. I felt unprotected and did not have anyone to turn to. My father would not save me from my mother, and my mother would not save me from my father.

I always wondered why my sister was safe. Why daddy never screamed at her for not doing daily chores correctly? Why mommy always hugged and kissed her, but never me? I truly loved my little sister because she never endured the treatment from mommy and daddy as I did. I thought she was the perfect child. She seemed to receive the most love from our parents. She never liked to go outside and play. She only wanted to be inside doing her homework. Mostly, she was a child who was seen and not heard. I have to say that she was a sweet child. For most of our childhood, my sister lived a life of happiness, whereas I lived a life of pure hell. How could this stark contrast of our upbringing be, especially since we both lived in the same house?

When I was 10, it really made no sense to me why my sister was treated so differently. I was a good girl too. However, when I look back now, I believe my mother resented me being born because the beginning of my life meant the ending of hers. My mother married my father when she was 17. She never got to experience going to parties, staying out late, or even hanging out with the girls at the movies or the mall. She was a married, pregnant teenager, who married out of obligation instead of love. Adult life and responsibilities came so rapidly, when she married my father. I certainly believe that every time my mother saw my face, it reminded her of all the things she was not able to engage in, or opportunities she missed out on in her young life. She did not experience the joy of maturing into adulthood or going to college because of me, so maybe that is why she treated me terribly. I certainly have asked myself why, quite a few times.

From the outside looking in, we were the perfect family and our home was the perfect place to be. Every kid on the block wanted to come over and play with us. We had the best toys, swings in the front yard, and a swimming pool. We also had a basketball court and plenty of snacks to share. My friends would often say, "I wish your mommy and daddy were my mommy and daddy." They would always tell me how nice my mom and dad were. Hearing all of those comments as a child would just make me cry because I knew the truth. The truth is my mom hated me and my dad molested me. I could not tell anyone. So, I kept quiet in misery and still sought their love and approval. I believed if they saw how special I was, they would not abuse me anymore. I kept trying to please them, but to no avail.

Sometimes, when daddy would signal me to come in his direction, I would just freeze up. He would tell me how I was, "daddy's favorite girl," as he touched me on the private areas of my body. Each time I sat on his lap, I was so afraid and never knew what to say or do. I was terrified, because each time he touched me, he threatened to kill me, if I told mommy. You know what? I believed him. I was a 10 year-old, whose mind was completely devastated. I would cry, thinking, oh, God, why is this happening to me? What have I done to him to deserve this? Why me, God?

When the molestation began, at first, the touching was not that often. Daddy began to call me more often to come to him. On the day he called me into the living room; it became clear that what my daddy was doing was wrong. I saw the bed spread stretched out on the floor. That was the beginning of a new nightmare.

A LOVE LETTER

Dear Readers,

It is my privilege to share the dramatic accounts of my life and others around me. Out of respect for their privacy, I have changed the names in our stories to protect the identity of those who were once victimized. Often, tremendous shame and guilt follow a person who has been abused--verbally, sexually, or physically. God has delivered me; therefore, I am transparently sharing my story so that you may become free of your past. This letter is for those desiring to move forward in obtaining a great future.

My story is a story of love, confusion, joy, anger, peace, and poor decision-making. You will see the consequences, as well as the fruits of my labor. You will see the ups and downs, certainties and uncertainties of my life. You will see my Christian walk as I learned to fight to create a new life of meaning and purpose. My story will provide you with information expected to challenge you in your thinking. If you have been victimized in any way, or know someone who has been victimized, I am challenging you to put the past behind you.

We all have to make peace with our past, learn from it, set new goals for our lives, and move forward. No, it is definitely not as easy as it sounds. I hope that through my testimonials you realize that healing needs to occur and that it begins with forgiveness. We have to forgive the victimizer, forgive God, and most importantly, forgive ourselves. God has restored me, and He will restore you too. Yes, my friends, God does have purpose in our pain.

Valerie H. Lane

MY PRAYER

I pray for each one of you right now, in the name of Jesus! I pray for courage, boldness, and transformation in your lives. God, please, create in them a clean heart, that they may see your goodness. Father, it is not by accident, that they are reading this book right now, it is truly by design. Father, you know what each and every one of them stands in need of. Your desire for them is to be free from their past, free from sin, and free from guilt and shame. I pray that this book causes lost souls to draw toward you. You are marvelous and are a Healer! It is in Jesus' mighty name that I pray, Amen!

IT'S NOT ABOUT YOU
Chapter 1

What is the first thing that comes to your mind as you read the following, italicized statement? *"It's not about you!"* Has anyone ever made that statement to you? I wonder if you resented the person for making that remark or if your reply was similar to mine. Here is what I used to say, "What do you mean it is not about me? After all the years of abuse, anger, frustration, disappointment, and heartaches, oh yeah, it is all about me. I am the one who was abused. I am the one who cried all night. I am the one who has been praying constantly for God to do something with me. Now, you are telling me it is not about me. Please, help me out here. If it is not about me, then who is it about?"

I have great news! There is an answer, but it took me years to figure it out as I began to see things clearly. I pray that what took me years to figure out, will take you less time. Once you make up your mind to do something different and to think differently that is when God does His best work. God spoke to me so clearly one night. He said, "Valerie, honey, yes you may have been used, abused, confused, aggravated, and frustrated but understand, it's not about you! Somewhere in your process, you began to lose hope. But dry your tears because it was all for such a time as this."

You see, my ministry was birthed out of my misery. To break it down for you, if I had not gone through what I went through, it would be very hard to relate to what God has called and anointed me to do. I was able to find God in the process. Perhaps, you may think your situation is so overwhelming that you might as well give up. The devil is a liar!! Genesis, 50:20, says, "But as for you, ye thought evil against me; but God meant it unto good, to bring to pass, as it is this day, to save much people alive." In other words, no matter what circumstances or misfortunes that have occurred, God can bring light to darkness. He can unscramble the mess and bring a clearer vision. He can use those negative experiences to develop your character. Why does God do that? The reason being is that there is a definite purpose in your pain.

Have you ever asked God where He when all those terrible things were happening to you? Psalm 139:8, says, "If I ascend up into heaven, thou art there: if I make my bed in hell, behold, thou art there." You have to stretch your hands and reach for God's hands no matter where you are. Why? What does God promise us? Isaiah, 26:3, says, "Thou wilt keep him in perfect peace, whose mind is stayed on thee: because he trusteth in thee." So what do we have to do? According to Psalm 1:2, "But his delight is in the law of the Lord; and in his law doeth he meditate day and night."

God can declare a mistrial or render a not guilty verdict even when we have participated in sinful acts, voluntarily or involuntarily. He does not throw us away because we have made errors in judgment or actions. In other words, he justifies us. However, we do have to confess and repent, and we can't go back in the wrong direction. Romans 8:1, says, "There is therefore now no condemnation to them which are in Christ Jesus, who walk not after the flesh, but after the Spirit." Be not deceived my brothers and sisters, the, "now no condemnation," refers to those who have accepted the Lord and Savior Jesus Christ in their lives. It is only through Jesus that we can be freed from our sins, hurts, and experiences that have us bound. "Now no condemnation," also covers whatever has gone wrong or whatever you may have done wrong; nevertheless, God is saying it is over. He says, "I forgive you, forgive yourselves, and forgive those who have hurt you."

The bottom line, my friend, is that despite all the hell you have gone through and will go through, "it is not about you!" John 10:10, says, "The thief cometh not, but for to steal, and to kill, and to destroy: I am come that they might have life, and that they might have it more abundantly." If we keep it real, it was not until after all hell seemed to break loose in our lives that some of us started seeking God for ourselves. Please understand that regardless of how much control you may think you have, "it is not about you!" It is about your purpose here on this Earth at this appointed time.

Ask God why you are here and what your purpose is. If you are still here on Earth that means your purpose has not been fulfilled. I was so caught up in my failures that I could not see my success. Success is not always synonymous with wealth, prestige, or accomplishments. Success can come in the forms of healing and restoration. What is it that God has for you to do that you are not doing?

GETTING PASS YOUR PAST
Chapter 2

I am committed to helping others to make peace with themselves concerning their past. There is nothing more tormenting than feeling as if you are unworthy, no matter how much good you do. I know, because I am writing from all the experiences that plagued my life while performing good works. God has given me a recipe that has allowed me to make peace with my past. Therefore, I would count it as robbery of God's grace, not to extend these ingredients to you so that you too may be freed from your past. James 4:17, says, "Therefore to him that knoweth to do good, and doeth it not, to him it is sin."

Growing up as an abused child, from ages 10 to 20, weighed more heavily on my decision-making than I would ever care to admit. I thought once I left home at 20, I would finally be alright. I didn't know the effects of the abuse would eventually poison every area of my life. With all of the trials I experienced, I considered my life to be worthless and unproductive.

I had an enormous amount of anger, bitterness, shame, hurt, unforgiveness, and resentment. Rages of insecurity and anxiety would erupt daily in my mind. My heart had grown cold and was a storage house for pain. To make matters worse, I had to admit that I was angry with God. I questioned Him on various issues of my life. Oh, by the way, it is alright to let God know you have issues, even when it concerns Him. Be honest and tell Him how you feel. You have to remember that God is omniscient, so He already knows. Communing with Him helps you to establish a closer relationship with Him. You have to want to be in fellowship with the Lord in order to get closer to Him.

Somewhere in life, I longed for others to share my pain. As I searched for help to understand my pain, I began realizing the world around me was full of people who shared burdens of grief from similar experiences. They were being held back from succeeding, because they allowed their past to keep them in bondage. It does not matter whether you are black, white, young, old, educated or uneducated; many have allowed what others have done to them to prevent them from moving forward to obtain a better quality of life.

After a major breakthrough in my walk with Christ, I decided to open myself up to God's call to minister healing to hurting people. I have dedicated my life to helping others face their past and move towards the future God has for them. Remember, my struggles started at home first. I did not realize that those times initiated my valley experiences. It was in those struggles that God began to equip me for the work in the ministry. Seeing people repeat abusive habits they vowed never to repeat is unfortunate, and sadly, more common than I care to admit. Bad habits are sometime generated from what I believe are the dynamics of generational curses. Some may say, "It is in their DNA."

All I am saying is that God can deliver you from any situations you may be encountering right now. Make the choice to ask Him for that deliverance.

A DECADE OF ABUSE
Chapter 3

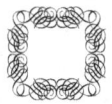

I remember the events of the abuse as if they happened yesterday. My mom came and told my sister and me that she was going to Miami, Florida with her cousin to visit her brother. She said she would be back in three days. I remember the night she left. My dad called me in the room to get in the bed with him. He began to fondle my breasts and touch my private area. At the age of 10, I was not sure what was going on. I was not aware that those moments were going create, what I called, a life of total hell for years. I remember being scared and ashamed. My grades in school started to drop, bur amazingly, no one ever asked why.

My mom would say I was stupid and I would never amount to anything. At the age of 13, I was attracted to anyone who would pay me some attention. I was told I was fast and a hot, little girl who wanted to be grown. That was really not the case. I was really angry and a hurt little girl who did not have a clue about what was happening.

Like so many adults who have experienced abuse, as well as neglect as a child, I was constantly trying to figure out what was wrong with me and why I was so different. In other words, why me? I did not experience joy in my childhood. Much of my childhood was broken because of the mental abuse, physical pain, and suffering I experienced. I can say, with assurance, that the pain has been traced back to my home life with my parents. I came to realize that we were not the perfect family, as everyone thought. Having a swing set, pool, basketball goal, skates, and bicycles created envy among my friends, but it still did not make us perfect. We were hiding secrets. If others were made aware of those skeletons, I was convinced that shame would soon follow. What goes on in this house, stays in this house! That was the statement that I came to know as the cover-up syndrome.

As I look back now, I realize how much my dad would play my mom against me. As a manipulation strategy, he would have her to focus on how bad I was to detract from how abusive he was. He was very convincing. For years, I cried myself to sleep hoping that somehow someone would know or even ask me what was wrong.

It was very hard because as a child, I thought parents were supposed to love and protect you. I kept thinking, "Why me?" Those two words were my general response to life. When we went to family functions, my dad would always be the jokester. He knew how to make everybody laugh and have a good time. As I watched him provide laughter for others, I would stare and concoct mental plans of what I could do to hurt him. I thought of ways of destroying his perfect image. I wanted revenge! I wanted to expose my dad's abusive acts, but who would believe me? He was the life of the party. Surely, my mom would take his side and think I was making up lies on my father. So, I kept quiet.

Growing up and wanting to go out and have fun was a struggle. Every time I asked my mom if I could do something or go anywhere, she always told me to ask my dad. So, my interactions in childhood always seemed to come with a price. Whenever I wanted to go out on dates, my father forced me to have sex with him first. I was very angry at my mom growing up because I thought as a mother she should have known something was wrong. I pondered so many questions and thoughts in mind during those times. How can a mom not know what is going on with her child? A mother is supposed to have intuitive thoughts. Mothers are just supposed to know. I often wonder why my mother did not save me.

Despite the abuse, they faithfully took us to church. Every second and fourth Sundays, I sang on the Sunbeam choir. As I got older, I moved to the young adult choir. Each Sunday, I heard about the God that everyone said we should serve. I remember praying as a kid and asking God to help me to be a good child so my mom would love me. It seemed like the more I prayed, the worse the situations became. Have you ever felt like that? The more I asked God to show up, the further away from me He seemed to be.

I can remember vividly listening to the messages of God's love, but I was hiding behind so much pain. That made it so hard to even hear God. It is amazing the many people in churches today hear the Word of God, but their pain causes the Word of God to fall on stony ground. What I mean is they go to church in turmoil, God speaks His Word through the pastor or worship songs, and they go back home the same way they came in; still in despair and broken with no relief. Mark 4:15, says, "And these are they by the way side, where the word is sown; but when they have heard, Satan cometh immediately, and take away the word that was sown in their hearts."

Life did not get any better when I moved out of my parents' home. I left that abusive home only to end up in abusive relationships. My first job was at Kroger, as a cashier. My dad said I should try to work at Campbell's Soup or McDonald's. I did not see myself on anyone's soup line or serving food. My parents would utter the words, "You think you are too good to work at those places, you will never do any better." Each time I would hear those words from them, something pierced my soul. I asked to go to a junior college because they said I was not smart enough to go to a real college. They both laughed and said they would not waste any money sending me to anybody's college. I worked at Kroger for a year and decided that there had to be something better that I could do.

I wanted so badly to prove to my mom that I was a good person, so I put in an application at a bank. I remember telling them both I applied, and they both laughed and said, "Who would hire you?" Two weeks later, I received a call from Citizens and Southern Bank about an interview. I was so excited and thought surely my parents would be proud of me. I went on the interview, and one of the bank's representatives called back within three days saying I got the job as a teller. Oh my God, finally something seemed to be working in my favor! I could not wait to tell my parents, thinking they would be happy for me. When I did, I only ended up getting disappointed again. "My God, why can't I get it right?"

At the age of 19, I became extremely angry with God. Hearing the messages of love was excruciating during those times, but receiving the messages was even harder. I thought, "How could God love me and allow me to go through all this hell." I was taught that God makes provisions for His people. I didn't think I was special in His eyes. How can He love us and let little girls be hurt? I had so many questions. I felt so disappointed in God.

At this point in my life, I came to the conclusion that I was cursed by God, and that being alive was a mistake. After all, that is what my parents constantly told me. The anger escalated as I meditated on the thought that God was supposed to be a good God. He was not there to help me. So, I decided that I no longer wanted to live, and that suicide was my only option. I attempted to take my own life numerous times and failed. On many occasions, I would cut myself. I sliced my wrists with sharp razors and knives. I could only feel numbness in my soul. I did not even feel the pain as the blood poured out of the open wounds. I even tried to stab myself in the neck with a screwdriver, but, when that did not work either. I believed I had no other choice but to swallow a bottle of sleeping pills. After all of those failed attempts, I am still here. Your mind will make you think that the mess you are in is so bad, you just need to end your life. That is definitely a trick of the enemy.

TORE UP FROM THE FLOOR UP (PART 1)
Chapter 4

I am sure many of you have, at some point, heard the saying, "Tore up from the floor up." In many cases, it represents someone who is either intoxicated or unattractive. Of course, it is a slang statement that perhaps may be a little too extreme. I did not come to know the statement as representing any of the people I have mentioned above. However, I prefer the statement, "I need a check-up from the feet up." I can relate to that statement because it describes the need for us to evaluate our personality, motives, heart, and nature. Additionally, it is descriptive of someone who thinks that he or she is alright, but is in denial to the need to confront the past. You may think you have it altogether, but others may see that there are some elements in your life that need to be addressed.

That was definitely me. I was the church attendance queen. As an adult, I went to church every Sunday morning at 7 a.m. I thought if I came extra early God would be pleased with me for making such an early effort. However, I realized that God did not give me bonus points, or care if I arrived at 7 a.m. or 5 a.m., if my heart was not right. I thought I was good or somehow better than others because at least I went to church. That was far from the truth. Yes, I was in church Sunday after Sunday, but, at that time, nothing seemed to be changing. In fact, my life had taken several terrible turns, even while I sat faithfully in the pews.

I remember one night praying and telling the Lord that I did not like the way I was. "Please, change me, Lord!" I asked him that repeatedly. It seemed as if everything in my life had failed, and no matter what I started I could not complete. One day, my sister invited me to her church. At first, I was a little hesitant because I was unfamiliar with the church. I decided just to go for it. I decided that I would go after asking myself, "What do I have to lose?" How many of you have had those moments when it seems that the preacher was talking directly to you? That is exactly how I thought the first day I attended. I believe wholeheartedly that God used the associate pastor to minister to me, because he vividly spoke about the things that happened in my background. After that day, I decided to go back to that church. My sister and her best friend would sit in the third row from the front. At that time, I was only comfortable sitting in the balcony section of the church. Eventually, I moved to sit with them because after a while I thought that if I continued to sit in the balcony, I would not get any closer to God. I am amazed at the things we convince ourselves of to believe.

Of course, your seat choice is not a representation of how you feel about God. However, choosing to move closer to the altar made me feel like I had accomplished something for the first time in my life. I did not attend that church consistently, but when I was away, I felt as if I was missing something. After a year of coming and going, I decided to join and become a member. My sister was a bit shocked because although she introduced me to the church, she had not joined.

Once I became a member, I desired to become a part of every ministry in the church. Ironically, I was afraid to do anything. I used to observe other people who had been in church for a while and I always thought, "Lord, I want to be like them." Is there someone you have noticed who seems to have the "God thing" figured out? I desperately wanted to get in touch with God. I thought for a while that I was the only one in church who did not have it together. I remember crying when the choir would sing songs like, "Yes," "Order My Steps," "Stand," and "No Weapon." I wanted to know this God that could heal me from hurt and pain. Even though I was attending church on a consistent basis and was excited when God's Word came forth, I still felt as if I was too messed up for God to deal with me. Those feelings were not from the Lord. God brings comfort in painful situations. Those self-defeating thoughts and doubts were planted in my mind by the enemy; the one who wanted me to go back to a faithless place. James 4:4 says, "…know ye not that the friendship of the world is enmity with God? Whosoever therefore will be a friend of the world is the enemy of God."

I was in so much torment. It was like trying to climb over a wall that I could not see, but something inside would just not let me give up. Trying to commit suicide did not work, so I began to think that I must be here for a reason. To try and battle the negative thoughts in my mind, I began listening to sermons by T. D. Jakes. "Woman, thou Art Loosed," is what Bishop Jakes would emphasize. Those tapes were encouraging. I would also listen to tapes by Joyce Meyer, because she also endured sexual abuse as a child. I related so much to what she said in her testimonies. Her stories gave me hope. Both pastors spoke messages of God's love and grace. My pastor was also vital in speaking words of life into me. I am forever changed, because of the words God allowed those ministers to impart into His people. As I continued to listen to God's word, my life began to change. I was willing to do whatever it took to make a total change.

I went through my humbling experiences, and it was not easy. You see, I had everything going for me on the outside but I was tore up from the floor up on the inside. Whatever you don't confront from your past has a way of seeping into your future. So, it was my desire and prayer that God would clean me from the inside out. Be careful what you ask God for because He just might do it. Every Sunday, I would go to the altar crying and hoping God would say something to me. Each Sunday I would say, "I just need a Word, Lord. I just need to know that You know I am here. I need to feel Your love, God."

God seemed to be talking to everyone, but me. It seemed like the ministers would pray and lay hands on everyone else at the altar, except me. At one point I was mad because I thought in order for God to heal me, the ministers would have to physically touch me. I know now, that is so far from the truth. Some people will make you think that the only way you can get to God is through them. The devil is a liar! As I walked back to my seat, disappointed that no one prayed with me, the choir sang the song, "The Change Will Come," by The Wilmington Chester Mass Choir. I remember the young lady singing that song with such an anointing. I heard her say if I would pray about it, get up and go on my way, that I could then watch God change it. The last part of the song said the change was within me. When I heard those words, for the first time, I felt like God was speaking to me.

I went through life blaming everything and everyone for my failures, pain, abuse and the disappointments I experienced growing up. Yes, my parents did abuse me and they played an instrumental part of my dysfunctional life. I did not feel the love and connection that I should have had with my parents. I blamed them constantly for me being this way. No, I am not discrediting what you may be going through or may have experienced in your life, but I am saying that at some point you have to begin to take responsibilities for the actions you involved yourself in as a consenting adult. Horrific things may have happened to you but what are you going to do now? You are still here!!!! Those were also some tough realizations for me.

When I began to take what I just told you to heart, I decided to stop being the victim. Notice I said, I decided, that means that it was a choice. Deuteronomy 30:19 says, "I call heaven and earth to record this day against you, that I have set before you life and death, blessing and cursing:

therefore choose life, that both thou and thy seed may live." I decided to choose life, rather than death. My change came, but it was not overnight. It was a lengthy and often tedious process. In this fast-paced, microwave generation, some expect things to happen so quickly, but that's not always how God operates. I am not saying that God cannot change things in an instant, because, He can. I am just saying that we have to be encouraged, even when His timing seems lengthy. It is His choice on how long the process will take, but you can also draw a process out if you choose to walk in disobedience.

TORE UP FROM THE FLOOR UP (PART 2)
Chapter 5

Although I had so much going on in my life at the time, I desperately wanted to please my mom. Even as an adult, I wanted her to see that I was not a bad person. I wanted her thoughts, feelings, and opinions to change about me, but they didn't. I found strength in my son. He definitely served as an inspiration to keep going. If no one else loved me, I knew for sure that my son did. At the age of six, my little boy would always ask me if I was alright. He would follow up that question with a simple statement that melted my heart, "Everything is going to be okay, Mom." Sometimes, as much as we try to shield our kids from our drama, they often sense when something is wrong. As parents, we have to be careful what we say in front of our young, impressionable children.

Let me tell you a little story about a young man I was dating during this time. He was such a nice guy. The downside is that he was abusive at times. My desire for love enabled me to equate his violent actions as acts of love. I thought this was his way of showing me that he really cared. Have you ever thought that your significant other was just a passionate person and that those abusive forms of expressions were somehow

> "When obstacles arise, you change your direction to reach your goal; you do not change your decision to get there."
>
> Zig Ziglar

normal? To make matters worse, he was not even faithful to me. He dated other women, when I truly thought I was the only one. My mind rationalized and eventually convinced me that this relationship was acceptable. He accused me of being responsible for his cheating, so basically it was my fault. Deep down, I knew this relationship was not what I wanted, but little, nagging voices in my head kept telling me that this was all I deserved.

For a couple of years, I continued down this path with him until I lost it. I was riding in his neighborhood and spotted a car parked at his house. I just assumed the car belonged to a female. I walked in his house and immediately started throwing his items on the floor. I wanted to mess up his house really badly. Luckily, he was not even home at the time. He was at the store with a friend. As I look back on that incident, that was really an insane moment.

While I was seeing this man, I began attending conferences for women. I began to tell my story to others. I emphasized how hurt I was and what type of man I wanted in my life. I desired to be transparent about the events that had transpired in my life. I hoped attending these events would help me. Numerous women shared that it was necessary to sometimes keep quiet, observe, and listen. They stated that I could learn people's true character by patiently watching how they treat me. In other words, people can only pretend for so long before they show you who they really are. I wanted someone who was caring, affectionate, loved God, and loved my son. I came to realize that everything I said I wanted, were the exact traits the men exemplified. However, things changed and those characteristics dwindled after I became intimate with them.

I have dealt with issues in my life when it came to searching for love. I have traveled around the United States following my boyfriends. Although I heard the words of warning from the ladies, I still did not understand the wisdom of their words. I met yet another nice guy. He was a retired, professional baseball player who had his own business. I am moving on up now, I thought. Oh, he is the one! I just knew he was it because he was a churchgoer. He even told our pastor that he was going to marry me. Although he attended church every Sunday, he had a dark, violent side. On the weekends, he would take his frustrations out on me. He would hit me in the head with his baseball bat. Once, he stuck my head in the commode.

Quite often, I would have to pick him up because he said his car was in the shop. He would use my car and drop me off at work. Within six months, he moved into my house without me realizing what was going on. I'm sure you are thinking, "How could she not see what was happening?" I got myself into this situation and did not realize what was happening until it was too late.

To make a long story short, my VCR, jewelry, and other items began vanishing from my house. It was very strange but I did not put too much emphasis on the missing items. One night, I received a phone call from a grocery store asking me to verify a check that someone was trying to cash in my name. I let the clerk know that I did not write any checks and that my checks were stolen. It still did not register with me that this guy had stolen my checks. Instead of asking him, I called my best friend and told her what happened. She was adamant that he was doing drugs, but I was in denial. How dare she accuse him of such things, I thought. I have never been around anyone doing drugs and did not know what signs to look for. Apparently, my friend was sure that he exhibited the traits of a drug addict because she was a recovering drug addict herself so she saw the clues. Oh my God, what have I gotten myself into?

I felt so helpless. I lost complete control of my life and everything in it. I thought I had it going on. I had a great job, my own dream home, good credit, and my son was in a private, Christian school. Although this man treated my son as if he was his very own, I made sure that my son did not witness the abuse. I sent my son to visit his dad for the summer. For the next couple of months my life was ruined, all because I looked for love in all the wrong places. This guy even set my bed on fire.

Calling the police did not help the situation. He was such a convincing actor that after he spoke with the police they seemed to not take my claims seriously in the legal sense. The police advised me to report him to the pastor of our church. I called several more times when his violent incidents would arise. Each time, the police indicated that because the man stayed at least 24 hours at my house that this house was just as much his as it was mine. He would take my car and disappear for days. My friends were no longer talking to me, mainly because he was making sexual advances toward them. My family wanted nothing to do with me because they could not believe how naïve I was. Honestly, I could really understand how each of them felt. They had valid reasons to feel the way they were feeling.

I continued to find evidence that he was responsible for taking my jewelry. I found tickets from a local pawn shop. I worked at a credit union and my account was in the negative because he wrote thousands of dollars of bad checks in my name. So, I ended up losing my job that I worked at for 10 years. I did not press charges because he promised he was going to pay me back and plus he threatened to kill me. I was so scared all the time. I prayed that it would all be over soon and that he would leave me alone.

I thought, what else could go wrong? One Monday afternoon, I received a phone call at work indicating that I needed to pick up my Infinity J30 car. My car was left abandoned with the speakers missing. Shortly after that call, he called me from the hospital to tell me that someone shot him several times in my car. At that time, I really did not care what was going on with him. I just wanted to know where my car was. My car was a total loss.

There was blood everywhere. I was so hurt that I allowed someone to come in and do so much damage to my life.

Things just went from bad to worse. I lost my car, my job, and I did not have a safe place to stay. This was definitely a valley experience. No matter what I did, things were not working. Now, I was ready for a change. I wanted to experience God, not through someone else's eyes, but through my own. I wanted to hear His voice. While all of this was going on, I still went to church. Someone would either pick me up or let me borrow their car.

The defining moment of this relationship ended in near death. He viciously beat me once again and threw my body in the road, leaving me for dead. A woman found me all bloodied and battered. She bought a Greyhound ticket and sent me to the address that was listed on my driver's license. When I arrived in my hometown of Sumter, South Carolina, I was so embarrassed. How was I going to return home like this? Surely, my family would be ashamed of me for letting this happen. Until this day, I do not know who that woman was. She truly was used to save my life.

During this time in my life I did not know whether I was coming or going. Every day, I cried and petitioned God. I watched the Trinity Broadcast Network (TBN) every morning, afternoon, and night, trying to get a word from God. I read my Bible day and night. Have you ever felt like no matter what you do, nothing seems to be working? It seemed like God was speaking to everyone but me. Things seemed to be going good for everyone else, but nothing really changed for me until I started to deal with me. For years, I suppressed everything that happened to me while growing up, and pretended that I was alright. Through all the nonsense I went through, I realized that God was there the whole time even when I felt alone. I know that God was trying to get my attention and He had to allow those things to happen so He could mold my character. Philippians 3:14, says, "I press toward the mark for the prize of the high calling of God in Christ Jesus." It took many years of falling down and getting back up before I realized that regardless of what it may have looked like at that moment, God had my back. The same applies to you. If you let go and let God, you will realize He is, and always was here all the time.

IDENTITY THIEF
Chapter 6

Identity theft is growing rapidly. I have heard countless stories on the radio and television regarding this senseless act. Imagine for a moment that you are about to make a big purchase with your credit card and the cashier keeps sliding the card through as though something is wrong with the machine. You are waiting patiently because you know there is not an issue with your card because you have excellent credit and a big maximum balance. I have heard that every 30 seconds someone's identity is stolen.

There are programs to protect you from identity theft. I once saw a company on television that guaranteed they could protect you from identity theft. In fact, according to the television commercial, the company's representatives were so sure of their abilities that they sent a truck down the road with a real social security number plastered on the sides. As I sit and think about the millions of people who may have been victims of identity theft, I often wonder what and how much it cost them to get their lives back on track.

As I was sitting and writing this book, I thought about another identity being stolen every second of the day—OUR SOULS! Yes, our Christian identity can be stolen. The enemy is roaming around trying to destroy our faith and belief in God. Satan does that through tempting us. Satan wants us to concentrate on the here and now rather than our eternal reward in heaven. He baits us by deception and convinces us to believe that he has more than God is willing to provide. He did the same thing to

Jesus in the garden. So, why do we think we are exempt from trials or tribulations, if Jesus was without sin and went through hard times?

I was doing all the right things. I was an avid churchgoer, choir singer, prayer warrior, and a meditator of God's Word. I believed in the Word of God. However, my actions showed otherwise. There was a battle going on inside my mind. The devil does not take into consideration that you are in church on Sunday mornings and Bible study on Wednesday nights. His main objective is to rob you of knowing who you are in Christ.

Let us talk about the battlefield within the mind. Sometimes, it seems that our faith is strong, as long as everything is going the way we planned. As soon as there is a problem, no matter how big or small, our faith seems to waiver. I am not saying that this happens to everyone. I am certainly talking from the experiences of others and myself. The battle really starts when it seems that everything is breaking loose in your life, and you cannot figure out why God is taking his sweet time. It sounds harsh. I am sure many of you have thought this about God a time or two in your life. Then all of the confusing, little voices in your head scream questions contrary to the Word of God. Questions like, where is your God now? What are you going to do? You will never amount to much anyways! You have messed up so badly that God will not waste His time using you! The harsh statements and questions go on and on in your mind, until you begin to believe them and even repeat them to yourself. This also can be amplified by negative influences that you have allowed to be in your life. We have to be careful of who we surround ourselves with. Little by little, I allowed my identity to be stolen. It was the identity that God gave me when He formed me in my mother's womb. It was not yet known what I was to be, but I should have realized that my destiny involved working in God's kingdom.

I did not know I had purpose, so I questioned God as

well as myself. I thought, maybe I was too messed up. Maybe, God made a mistake when He made me. Maybe I should not even be here. Is there really a God? At the time, everything I touched seemed to fail. Even when you are going through, the enemy desires to trick you into believing you have no purpose. So many people emulate others, such as, celebrities, athletes, and professionals. So often, we are unable to be authentic because we desire the lives of others. Do not get me wrong, I am not saying that we should not have role models or express our God given talent. I am just saying that we should be who God called us to be. We never know what others had to go through to get where they are in life. Often, they have sacrificed their love for Christ and replaced His peace with fame, fortune, and money.

Who are we in Christ? Philippians 4:13, says, "I can do all things through Christ which strengtheneth me." Romans 8:37 says, "… in all these things we are more than conquerors through him that loved us." I am sure that you have heard these verses plenty of times, but they bear worthy of repeating, we are the head and not the tail; we are the lender and not the borrower.

How do we allow our mindsets to change? God gave us instructions in His word. Psalm 77:12, says, "I will meditate also of all thy work, and talk of thy doings." Philippians 4:8, says, "Finally, brethren, whatsoever things are true, whatsoever things are honest, whatsoever things are just, whatsoever things are pure, whatsoever things are lovely, whatsoever things are of a good report; if there be any virtue, and if there be any praise, think on these things." When we start to truly believe those scriptures, we are provided with strength and assurance that we can triumph regardless of the failures we have encountered.

I was very much a people pleaser. I wanted everyone to

be happy, regardless of how I felt. To combat negativity, I began surrounding myself with positivity—people, my surroundings, and the Word of God.

For those who think God has forgotten you, don't give up. Somewhere down the line, your identity was stolen and it is time to take the necessary steps to get it back. Not only get it back, but secure it within Christ. To do so, you must pray and ask God to show you who you are, as well as your purpose for being here on Earth. You may not get your answer quickly, but you will begin to realize you do have purpose. Do not allow the tactics of the enemy to steal your joy or your peace. Stay in the Word of God because He will shield you from all the fiery darts that are being thrown to steal your identity. Meditate on the promises of God for your life.

What is it that you love or enjoy doing? Is there something you would love to do, even if you don't get paid for it? For me, it is helping people identify their inner beauty. I really enjoy seeing people smile. Not artificial smiling, but smiles that can brighten someone's life at a glance. I will never forget, I was walking out of a church service and a young girl about 13 years old walked up to me and said, "Miss Val, every time I look at you, you are smiling and it keeps me going, whatever you do, keep on smiling." Can you believe a 13- year-old said that? On another occasion, a young boy, about eight years old, came up to me and told me that I was always smiling. I simply replied to him that he should too. The reason I am mentioning this is because sometimes we look for God in the big stuff, and God is saying, I am also in the small stuff. You never know, your smile may change how you see the world and perhaps how the world sees you too. Smile!!!

A SMILE

This is a story, a story of regret
I write this tale so you won't forget
A tale of a broken heart
Past o'er time after time
'Til one day it decided it had had enough
It wanted to leave all the pain behind
No person would ever share their love
Not even a little touch
No one would ever give a smile
Just a smile, but it meant so much
If anyone had she would have gone on living
but I was too busy, that was my reason
This heart had walked three miles

Looking longingly just for one smile
She stopped at a bridge
No smile to be found
She calmly looked down
Soon death would come round
The very next day
That dear heart was found
It was smashed in the sea
Within it, no trace of love could be found
all that heart needed was a smile

But hundreds of people passed by her all the while
I often see that girl's face in my dreams
What if a smile on my face to her had been se
But it wasn't-
I just looked down with a frown
What could I have done with my friends all around?
Could I have helped that girl not to drown?
All she wanted was a smile—
A smile that I am now happy to give
A smile I shall share as long as I live
--Anne Sherman

DYSFUNCTIONAL FAMILIES (PART 1)
Chapter 7

It never ceases to amaze me that there are so many people hurting daily. Oftentimes, they do not even know why they are hurting. They just know that they feel a sense of awkwardness, or that there is a deep hole within their souls. Sometimes, they may even feel that they do not quite belong or fit in. When I think back to my childhood, I still find it amusing that everyone in my community deemed my family as being the perfect family. After 33 years, it was brought to my attention that perfection did not accurately describe who we really were as a family. We just knew how to hide our dysfunction from the public.

Mostly, the people I meet on a day-to-day basis are dealing with some type of dysfunction. I met a young lady a few years ago in a training session, and we talked about why we were both attending the training. I expressed to her that I had been hurt in so many relationships. I also told her that I'd, been abused, both sexually and verbally, in my childhood. I told her that it was my goal to help prevent others from having to go through what I went through in life. To make matters worse, I became a victim of domestic violence in my adult life. I shared my entire story with that young lady. On the final day of training, she began sharing her story with me, and I found parallels in our stories.

When I heard her speak of the events of her life, I knew that she was indeed a powerful lady who unknowingly had purpose. She grew up in an abusive household. In her case, her dad physically, emotionally, and verbally abused her mother. In the midst of the physical altercations, she was always the solution. In other words, the violence would not stop, unless she jumped in the middle of the yelling and the punches. This went on for years. After each incident, she would pray for God to help her family.

In her early 20s, she admitted to being afraid of confrontation. As a result, she began to accept the attention from men, even if it was unhealthy. She felt that if she complied or cooperated with them, they would provide her with a touch of comfort, rather than a punch like her father would give her mom. Seeking attention in the wrong places is how she coped with the challenges and fears she endured from her childhood.

When she felt the men becoming angry, she became even more frightened. She was afraid that if she told them to leave her alone they would kill her. One day she made up her mind that she was going to express to a guy that she was no longer comfortable seeing him anymore. He spent a considerable amount of time showing up where she was; even going to the extent of traveling great distances. Although, in her gut, she knew something was not right with this picture, she kept silent.

When she finally got up the courage to tell him that she did not want to see him anymore, before she could even finish her statement, the unthinkable happened. He picked her up and carried her over his shoulder into an unoccupied room at a college. Before he began to assault her, he cut the lights off in the room. He used one arm to put her in a headlock, and the other arm around her rib cage squeezing as tightly as he could.

She cried uncontrollably, while trying her best to wiggle her body so that it could loosen the grip. However, that did not work. This went on for a considerable amount of time. There were multiple screams in her throat, but none would be vocalized for others to hear. In the midst of this ordeal, she thought of the abuse in her home as a child. She was frightened that if she screamed or yelled out, he would kill her. She stopped moving for a moment, hoping he would stop. She was close to losing consciousness at one point, but God had a different plan in mind. On her last attempt to break free, she put all her strength into a grunt. It was quite unbelievable. With that last push, his arms moved from her so easily. She knew right then that it was definitely through no strength of her own, and that it was God who allowed her to escape. She literally felt His presence come alongside her to rescue her. Nonetheless, she was still too afraid to call the police. The guy ran behind her saying he was sorry and that this was not him. She could barely look at him, but when she did look back, while running through the parking lot looking for her car, she noticed that his face looked distorted.

She began looking over her shoulder even more within the next two weeks. She did not know if or when he was going to show up again. She had no other choice but to go to the police. Ironically, he followed her to the police station and threatened to kill her if she reported him. She thought back to her mother who never called the police on her father. At that moment, she realized that she had to do something different. She knew that she could not endure his violence any longer.

I noticed that as she told me her story, tears streamed down her face. It was at that moment that I realized she was carrying and holding onto the guilt and shame of what happened that tragic night. Until that time, she never shared the details of that story with anyone.

Once she gave her life to Christ, several years later, she began to speak about the things that she suffered. She spoke about the violence in her childhood and her experiences in her adult relationships. After listening to her stories, I asked her if she had ever received any type of professional counseling. She said she had not spoken to a professional, she just deals with it. In other words, she tried to avoid discussing the horrific events of her life. Her way of dealing with life was not to deal with it and to consume herself with work or projects. She did not realize that a cycle was being repeated. She would meet and date guys who were abusive like her dad. We both seemed to have attracted abusive men in our past. Sometimes, we look for love in all the wrong places, not realizing that we attract what we have not dealt with. Your past can heavily influence who you are as a person and also who you choose to love or socialize with.

Our purpose for attending that training was not only

to help ourselves, but also to seek help for others. Our logic is that if we can get information, we can somehow help others out of their situations. So, regardless of what we have been through in life, we must be aware that we must make a difference in the lives of others. To a certain extent, you can only help as far as your pain will allow. In other words, if you refuse to deal with your issues, your pain eventually could spill onto whomever you are trying to help. Although your intentions may be pure, you have to be honest and assess where you are in life.

After several weeks of talking to this young lady, I invited her to church. I also invited her to participate in the Making Peace with your Past support group. This support group helps people understand how dysfunction in their family impacts who they are today. It is my belief that when you get sick and tired of being sick and tired, you are willing to do whatever it takes to get a different outcome. She agreed to come to church and to participate in the group. During the support group, she laughed, cried, and released hurt, anger, and issues that she was holding onto for years.

After she went through her process, she became a much better person. She began to see herself differently, when dealing with the issues of her past. I have learned that change is not always easy. You know the optimistic, proverbial phrase, "When life gives you lemons, make lemonade." Regardless of the circumstances that may have taken place in your life, be determined to make it. Luke 1:37, says, "For with God nothing shall be impossible." I am so thankful that God has the final word. He has a way of plucking weeds out of your life and replanting you with seeds of righteousness. He can, will, and shall make you brand new, if you trust Him.

DYSFUNCTIONAL FAMILIES (PART 2)
Chapter 8

I want to share a story about a guy named Keith and many of you may relate to his story. Keith was 60 and about six feet tall. He had four missing teeth in the front of his mouth. He always spoke of his dream of driving 18 wheeler trucks. When Keith and I first met, he was reluctant about sitting among a group of people discussing his personal issues. At the conclusion of the Making Peace with Your Past interest meeting, Keith realized that he would indeed benefit from attending the support group sessions. He just needed to take his focus off being the oldest in the group.

On the first night of our support group, he was very quiet and was not really engaged in the conversation. It often takes time for new members to open up and share any information. Trust has to be developed. It was obvious that Keith was not quite ready, so we gave him time.

I could tell that Keith felt empathy for a young lady who spoke about her father not being a part of her life. In tears, she spoke of how he left her at an early age and never came back. She longed to be with him. She found him, when she got older. Unfortunately, he still did not want anything to do with her. I noticed that as the young lady talked water began to fill Keith's eyes. He began apologizing to the young lady for not being a good dad to her. This seemed strange at first, until he began to share his story with us.

Keith talked about what it was like growing up as a

child. He emphasized that no one liked him, not even his family members. He always felt unattractive and had to endure people calling him names. As a way of fighting back and feeling self-worth, he dated and had children from multiple women. When he shared that news with us, I could tell that he was not bragging. He was not proud of being with all those women. In fact, he was hurting because of the guilt and remorse of not being a part of his older children's lives. Keith desperately wanted to meet them and apologize for not being there.

When Keith was a little boy, his mom refused to let him spend time with, or talk to his father. He would often beg her to let him call his father. When he would ask her, she would beat him out of frustration. Keith grew up in the country so when he would go out and play with other kids, he would get picked on for not having a daddy. One day, at the age of nine, Keith, finally got his wish. His father came to the house to pick him up. What was so amazing to Keith is that his mother allowed his dad to come into the house. His father told him that he would come back to visit him. However, that never happened. His father did not keep his promise.

Keith experienced heartbreak and a range of other emotions, including anger. The anger was not just directed at his father, but he was also angry at his mother. That anger followed him into adulthood. At the time, he did not understand where it stemmed from. Keith vowed that he would never be like his father; however, he demonstrated similar attributes when it came to rearing his children. Sometimes in life, the very thing (or person) we vowed never to become, we end up becoming. Keith did not financially or emotionally support his older children. He did have a lot of contact with his youngest son who was in high school. He was allowed a short amount of time with his son because of a visitation order.

Keith wanted to meet the rest of his children but he thought they probably hated him, and that it was too late to have a relationship with them. The guilt overtook his life. Keith noticed that his youngest son also had anger issues. Keith could not understand why his son was so angry because in his mind, he was doing right by his son because he had some contact with him.

After a few sessions, Keith acknowledged that he was repeating the same cycle of dysfunction that plagued his childhood. Until that moment, he did not realize that he was carrying anger, resentment, and unforgiveness from his past. As much as we might say, "Oh, I am good," oftentimes, we probably are not. I am not saying that everyone is holding onto something from the past and repeating the same cycle. What I am saying is that we must evaluate ourselves and our lives to see if there are any patterns or connections to the past. During Keith's process, he became excited and wanted to confront the issues that were deeply embedded in his heart and mind, and caused guilt and shame. For once in his life, he was ready to move into his purpose and become the man that God called him to become. Keith was finally able to breathe several sighs of relief, as he was being set free from guilt. Romans 8:1, says, "There is therefore now no condemnation to them which are in Christ Jesus, who walk not after the flesh, but after the Spirit."

Keith completed all 10 sessions of the Making Peace with Your Past support group classes. Not only did he complete the classes, but he put into action, everything we discussed in the group. Keith contacted his daughter whom he has not heard from in years. Amazingly, she was also searching for him. Keith apologized to all of his children for not being there.

Establishing a relationship with his children, according to him, was the best thing that he has ever done in his life.

Guess what? Keith is now licensed and driving 18 wheelers across the United States. He even replaced those four front teeth with dentures. God's timing is surely amazing. He has a way of working things out for you. He cleans you up on the inside and then gives you a godly, spiritual glow to be reflected on the outside. His peace will change the way you walk, talk, look, and dress. Afterwards, His desire will become your desire. In turn, this will cause you to want to be a better representative and servant of Christ. When you make the decision to give your life to Christ and walk in His ways, your life will be different.

Here was a 60-year-old man who still was holding on to the pain of his father leaving him as a little boy. In his mind, his mother prevented a true bond from developing between father and son. There was a part of him that was still waiting for his father to return to his life, even as an adult. Your past can have a hold on your life. There are many people holding on to past hurts and failures, and God is waiting to set them free. To move forward you must make peace with your past. This does not mean that you have to like what has occurred. However, it does mean that you have to make a conscious decision to break those shackles of bondage. It does not matter where you are in your life today. It does not matter what circumstances you may be in. What does matter is that you have the power to change it. What are you going to decide?

Do not let your past poison anymore of your present or disrupt your future. It is becoming more apparent as I watch the nightly news that senseless acts of hatred and violence are occurring at astounding rates. People are killing infants and others for no apparent reason. Do you ever wonder what drives people to commit such heinous acts? Could something in their past be the catalyst behind their crimes or mindsets? I am not making excuses for criminal behaviors, I am just trying to understand why people do the things they do. I believe we have to examine a person's entire life to understand why they involve themselves in certain situations or commit certain acts. It's the same with us, if we do not deal with the issues now, they will affect us later.

THE HEDGE OF PROTECTION
Chapter 9

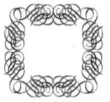

It was a Sunday morning and I was on my way to church. I had what some would call an epiphany. I began to recognize that there was a power operating in my life that would not allow me to give up. The scriptures that I learned as a child began to minister to my heart and mind. The sermons that I heard about the devil seeking to destroy my life started coming back to my remembrance. Now, it all makes sense. God really does love me! The devil was the true rival here—not God!

My healing started. Please understand that the healing did not start until I confronted and recognized I needed to be real with God about how I felt. I had to be honest about my feelings toward Him and toward myself. It is harder for God to reach us when we are in denial about how we truly feel. So, if He does show up, you will not even recognize He is there, because of your inability to be honest about your struggles. So with that understanding, I began giving God glory. I started with acknowledging that He had been there with me all the time, and He had a divine hedge of protection around me. Reflecting on this protection, I saw how God was present during the unsuccessful, suicide attempts. He did not allow me to die.

Getting a real understanding of the deity of God, how God sees me, and how much He loves me, (even in the abusive situations), made me realize I had purpose here on Earth. That is different from my previous perspective of asking, "Why am I here?" I began to ask God to show me who He really is and to show me my purpose of why I was created. When my mindset began changing, I finally began to see the world differently. Even more amazing is that I began to see myself differently. Step by step, I began reading and meditating on the Word of God. Sometimes, I would even giggle in amazement at each revelation I found through the scriptures that God was showing me. I had several light bulb moments. I began to realize why certain obstacles occurred. With each revelation, God began revealing who I am and His solutions for my life in the Word. The Lord is so awesome.

I began to understand the purpose God had placed in me, and it was not so much as me making things happen, it was me believing what He says in His Word. Matthew 6:33, says, "But seek ye first the kingdom of God, and his righteousness; and all these things shall be added unto you." It did not happen overnight. It was a process. I did not receive the clarity that I needed until God spoke to me in His still, small voice and stated, "For all the abuse you have been through, **it is not about you!**"

GETTING TO THE ROOT OF THE PROBLEM
Chapter 10

My husband and I had an opportunity to sit among a group of teenagers at a recreation center. The center served as a safe haven, one that provided emotional support and physical fitness activities. It became a place where teens could come for a few hours daily, just to get away from the trauma of what they were experiencing in their homes. As we introduced ourselves, I remember they looked at us as if we were peculiar people. I imagine that all too often they have had folks come and go without fulfilling their promises to help them. Nevertheless, we did not let their stares of doubt distract us from God's purpose.

We sat in a group circle and everyone introduced themselves. I will never forget the teen that came late to the circle. It was not the teen's tardiness that engaged my attention. It was the facial expression. This teen looked like a serious fighter. I am sure you know the look I am speaking of. It is the look someone gives that says, "I will attack anyone who says anything out the way." Almost immediately, I believed this was a shield to keep people away. I was not intimidated by the demeanor, nor, was I rattled by the oversized clothes, tightly snugged baseball cap, or black wristbands. Despite the disposition of anger, I engaged the teen anyway.

I received an unexpected surprise when the teen began to speak. I realized that this teen was a young lady. She did look tough and could be mistaken for a guy at first glance. I thought, My God, what in the world is going on with this girl? As we continued our discussion, she did not have much to say. The other teens shared their experiences of what was going on in their homes and at their schools. As I sat and listened, I realized how much these teens were hurting. They were battling severe issues and circumstances at such young ages. Sometimes, we think that what we are going through is bad and that no one else is having it so rough. Once you listen to the stories of others, you can always find a situation, problem, or life that seems to be worse than yours. Unfortunately, on that first introduction, the young lady refused to share what she was going through.

This first session was entitled, "Getting to the Root of the Problem." This topic was birthed out of a place of dismay. I grew tired of people repeating the same cycles and no one was attempting to provide them with help. It is a reality, and it saddens me that children are being affected by the choices of adults. No longer can we continue to use excuses like, this is how my momma was; my daddy was not there; this is just who I am. My husband and I thought we could help this group of teens to avoid repeating the mistakes and inappropriate actions of the adults they have interacted with.

As I proceeded to discuss how my past affected my adult life, the group circle grew silent. They looked in astonishment and were even a bit surprised at how brutally honest I was about the events of my childhood and adult life. I found out later that it was not so much of what I was saying, but was really about how relatable my story was to what they were going through. A wave of discussion ensued as my husband shared his testimony of overcoming the "street life."

As we concluded our first session, we promised the

teens that we would return on the following week. We gave them our phone number and stressed that they can call if they needed to talk to someone. I walked over to the young lady who I confused for a guy earlier. I said, "Young lady, I can feel your hurt. I know why you dress in those big, baggy clothes. You are trying to disguise yourself. You are hoping that you can hide your pain underneath the multiple layers of fabric. No matter how much you try to hide, God loves you. Please, take our number. When you are ready for change, please call us."

Since there was a great need to continue working with this group, my husband and I decided to expand to 12 weeks of group therapy. Our aim was to give the teens other options regarding how to move from where they are to where they want to be in life, (spiritually, socially, financially, physically, and academically). It was overwhelming at times, realizing that the teens were dealing with so much (from depression and low self-esteem to suicidal thoughts). Often, we as adults are not able to help those in need because we either do not know how or we are still trying to deal with our own issues. There were common denominators in each of their stories. Their parents were either on drugs or the teens were basically raising themselves.

One Wednesday night after bible study, I received a phone call. I was shocked to hear the voice on the other end. It was the young teen who was dressed like a guy from the group session. I was happy to hear from her, yet, my heart bled for her as she yelled at the top of her lungs. In her screams, I heard her utter words that led me to believe that she was going to hurt someone. She said she was about to set some people straight. I was trying to pinpoint exactly what was going on. I asked her to calm down and she became angry with me. "Why did I even call you?" she spouted in frustration. I stated to her that it was God who orchestrated our meeting and this phone call. "When you have been hurt so much by people it is sometimes hard to see any positive in others or in yourself for that matter," I said. She became much calmer so that we could speak candidly. I believe I was used by God to help this young lady. She was my assignment. I did not understand exactly what that meant or all that would entail. I was not sure what I was going to do or say to get her to look beyond where she was in life. However, I was certain that God was going to direct both of our paths. When God graces you with an anointing to help hurting people, he allows you to see straight through their pain. The difficult part comes in assuring hurting people who have been let down and feel defeated, that God still has a purpose for their lives.

As I walked with her at the beginning of her healing process, I encouraged her to start writing in a journal. This would be her written account of how God was ordering her steps. Her very first assignment was to write what she was feeling. In the meantime, I invited her to church with my husband and me. She said she would come, but she did not have a ride. All I needed to know is that she was willing to come. We agreed to pick her up on Wednesdays for bible study and Sundays for church service. God allows difficult things to occur in our lives to get our attention. When we are full of anger or are not keeping our eyes, hearts, and minds stayed on Him, we can often lose focus and reject what He is doing. We may see things as the worst events possible, while God sees them as opportunities for Him to show Himself powerful and mighty in our lives.

As time went by, she began to reveal why she was responding the way she was. She said her grandmother verbally abused her when she was a little girl and her uncle molested her. She went on to say how her mother would prostitute both her sister and her for drugs. She hated her mom for using them as sexual favors. She was placed in the foster care system because her mother was in jail on drug charges. To make matters worse, her dad was in prison for murder. As she revealed more of her story, tears ran down my face. It was not because I felt sorry for her because I understood where her attitude was coming from.

When you are hurting, even though you think you are hiding behind a mask, your inner feelings have a way of seeping out. Often, it comes out in the form of anger, as it did for this young lady. As I began to reassure her that God had a plan and a purpose for her life, she said, "God cannot use me, because I am so messed up." I assured this young lady that those thoughts were not of God and that they were designed by the enemy to distract her from what God wants to do in her life. When those negative, self-defeating thoughts come, we have to practice combatting those thoughts. Second Corinthians 10:5, says, "Casting down imaginations, and every high thing that exalteth itself against the knowledge of God, and bringing into captivity every thought to the obedience of Christ."

After getting passed the anger and attitude, she came to church more. In fact, she even invited a friend to church. We talked daily about how God loves her and how He sees her. I also understood she had a trust issue when it came to God. Therefore, my job was to sow seeds into her life and believe God for the water and the increase. As I continued working with her, I began to see a change. I saw God breaking down walls of anger, frustration, bitterness, and resentment in her life. He was taking away the hurt while restoring joy and peace. Although she was learning and hearing sermons on becoming a new creature, she continued to hide herself behind the baggy clothes. She was attending church consistently, but she still had an unapproachable, hardcore disposition. I encouraged her to keep studying the Word. She stated that she was reading the Bible every day. Our conversations with her became easier. She began asking questions about the Bible.

One night we had a church service, and she was on the program to read a poem. As she began to read aloud, the church became quiet and tears streamed down my face. I was so proud of her for participating. Even more so, it was her very own poem that she wrote. I knew at that moment that God was keeping His Word. He was bringing her out of bondage. In the poem, she spoke from her pain and how God came into her life. By that time, the entire church body was overcome with tears. That moment symbolized that the power of God can operate when you step out on faith.

My husband and I began to talk to her about the way she dressed and how she should carry herself as a young lady. We reminded her that she is a new creature in Christ. She no longer has to hide. She always said she would never wear a dress. Little by little, she began to let go of the oversized clothes. She admitted that she wore those clothes to hide her silhouette. She did not want anyone to notice her because of the past abuse. She was ashamed of her figure because she remembered what her mother allowed men and women to do to her just to get high. By wearing oversized clothes, she thought she was diverting attention away from herself.

I shared this story with you because so many people are hiding behind the pain, especially our teens. Instead of trying to impress the world with your outer appearance, let God clean you up from the inside out so the true beauty will come from within. The young lady later moved in with my husband and me, and we worked with her diligently. Amazing things happened to her. She had the opportunity to attend a college, tuition free. To God be the Glory! She became employed with an afterschool church program where she worked with young ladies. She encouraged them not to take the same path she took. She told them that her path was full of anger. She stressed the importance of letting God lead them into wholeness, regardless of where they are now.

Her story is incredible! No matter what your circumstances are, know that God loves you, and you do have purpose in this world. If you find yourself going through the same cycle over again, confront what it is so you can move forward into your purpose. God is amazing. Who would have thought that the young lady from the teens circle would come to live with us, become very active in church, and give back to the community through public speaking? If you make a decision to change and trust God He will help you and it can happen. It is not as hard as you think, it is a decision. Decide because God is waiting on you!

FOREVER THE VICTIM
Chapter 11

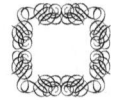

Have you ever been around someone who is constantly complaining? You may hear them say, "I am this way because of what happened to me." They may even say, "It is everyone else's fault." Maybe you have even said these statements. Perhaps, you too, have gotten comfortable playing the victim and letting the traumatic issues of your past prevent you from moving forward. Now, do not get me wrong, I am not belittling anything that you have gone through. Remember, I also went through serious events that have had devastating effects in my life. I have also engaged in this, "forever the victim" mindset, but through the grace of God, I now realize that I desire to be a victor.

Growing up in a small town, the Las Vegas mentality was applied, "What goes on in this house, stays in this house!" As I began examining the layers of my life, I realized that the dysfunctional tendencies in my household, and often in the neighborhood, were there the entire time. As I look back now, it was happening more than I even imagined. I remember families (including my own) that fought a lot. It was not just arguing and using profanity, but people were physically fighting so hard that the goal was to kill the other person. Thank God, I did not have to witness anyone dying after the physical blows and punches were finished. To us, as adults, we look back on our childhood and simply think that was the way of life. If someone hurts you, you hurt them back or get at him or her before he or she gets you. It was a "dog-eat-dog" mentality. When I see the new generation engaged in brawls over trivial matters, it breaks my heart.

For a majority of my adulthood, yes, I was a victim of many circumstances. Even when I had my son, I had grown accustomed to blaming everyone for my failures. Being a victim or blaming others somehow became engrained in me. I realized that I missed a big part of my son's life because my main issue or stumbling block was ME. I tried to be the perfect mom, but inside, I had a serious case of confusing emotions that left me with a, "poor me," attitude.

Speak to your circumstances. Genesis 50:20 says, "But as for you, ye thought evil against me; but God meant it unto good, to bring to pass, as it is this day, to save much people alive." I say to you, stop spending so much time trying to figure out why, and focus your attention on how your story can be used for the benefit of others. To those who have children or are planning to have children, please cherish every moment you have with them. Time does not go backward. You do not want to start a legacy of regret, shame, and guilt with your very own seeds. God can heal!

NO MORE DRAMA
Chapter 12

It is five o'clock in the morning, why am I even up? I have been constantly asking myself that question. I keep saying I need to write. There is so much I think people need to learn about themselves. I finally realize who I am and whose I am. It is really not about me. I have purpose and I have an assignment from God. Now what does that have to do with you? Well, let me tell you, there is so much drama going on in the world. Countless reality shows exist and are raking up in the numbers of viewership because of the drama. Those shows are becoming so popular that even some Christian shows have joined the reality club, and it is all because of D-R-A-M-A. Society sure seems to thrive on drama. They make money off it. They report it as if it is national news.

For a big portion of my life, although there was drama, I did not seem to enjoy it one bit. I have the honor of facilitating support groups\workshops entitled, "Making Peace with Your Past" and "Getting to the Root of the Problem." I did not realize these assignments were being birthed out of the drama of my life. Lord knows I had plenty of it in my lifetime.

I believe God led me to deal with my own drama. The more God shows you yourself, the less time you have to focus on other people's drama. That is because you realize that your life is full of issues, and you can only direct your attention at getting it together. I am sure glad that God offers agape love which is simply unconditional love. We need to offer that same kind of love to others. Of course it is natural to want to receive that kind of love from others, as well.

There is so much anger, bitterness, resentment, and unforgiveness that people are holding onto. I have been hurting for many years, blaming everyone but myself. Yes, I was abused from the time I was 10 until I left my parent's house, but there came a time in my life where I had to take accountability for my own actions. It was such a costly price to pay. I remember trying several times to commit suicide because I thought that my life had little value, and there was no use in me living any longer. Perhaps, some of you have also thought that way. All of the negativity that I endured coupled with striving to be something that I was not, and people pleasing, drove me into a walking grave. I was breathing, but I was not really living.

To God be the Glory!!! He saw this day, even when I did not think it would be possible. Never would I have imagined speaking life as opposed to death. Never would I have spoken of purpose. So, if you do not get anything else out of this book, please know that you have PURPOSE!!! No matter how bad you think you are at this moment or how bad things may have been in the past, God will take whatever you have gone through and turn it around for your good. What an Awesome God we serve!

I had to take that minute to give God the glory. I truly hope that I can help you overcome your circumstances too. It is important for you to know that you belong in the family of God. He will continue to work out the kinks in you, once you give your life to Him. I have learned to appreciate the good and the bad. I am confident that He will perfect what is unstable in my character.

Through mentoring teenagers and consulting with

adults, I realize that so many of us wear masks. Some of us wear them for a short period of time, while others have them on for extended periods of time. There is so much hurt and pain hiding behind the masks. It is also common to see mask-wearing Christians, I was one of them. Yes, I was in church every Sunday, crying at the altar, pleading for God to help me, and wondering why He cursed me. I had to be cursed, right? All of those bad things that happened to me as a child had to be characteristics someone who was indeed cursed. That was what I thought. In reality, that was not the truth. It just felt like that because I faithfully went to church and came home with suicidal thoughts. That was indeed a trick of the enemy.

Let me fast forward a little bit. God has cleaned me from the inside out. I am not perfect, but I have finally gotten to the point in my life where I understand, "it is not about me!" My heart bleeds as I watch the enemy attack families, marriages, relationships, children, and the body of Christ as an entity. We are expected to endure attacks, and the problem comes when we give up without a fight. I often come in contact with individuals who are in abusive relationships, have cheating spouses, or their children are joining gangs. Too often, Christians sit silently, saying nothing, just watching.

I wonder if morals and values are still important. The pretense that I see sometimes is astonishing. I see people pretending to love, pretending to care, pretending to have it going on, and pretending to keep it real. Pretending! Pretending! Stop the Pretending! Life is too short. Daily, we must make an effort to get ourselves together. We must stop playing the role of a Christian from a fleshly standpoint, and start serving Christ the way Jesus intended.

Once you begin to work on yourself, you will realize

that you are on assignment from God, even if you don't realize what that assignment is. In other words, whatever you have been through, if you are still here, God will use you to be someone else's answer to a problem. Perhaps, this equation will help you to realize that, Transformation + Time = A Process. What you have to do is renew your mind!

For many years, I had so many negative things said to me. I really believed that I was stupid, I would never amount to anything, and that I was a mistake. I believed those things to be true because I was told them as a little girl. When I became an adult, the voices were continuously repeating those negative thoughts in my head until I started operating in a self-defeated mindset. There may be many of you still holding on to the past, hoping and praying that the pain would just go away. I am here to tell you that until you confront and deal with what is holding you back, it will do just that, hold you back. As much as you try to act like you have it all together, your past has a way of seeping into your present.

When I initially started writing this book several years ago, I had no idea why it was taking so long to complete. When I started looking back over my life, it was painfully obvious that a great deal of my problems existed because I always started something but never completed it. On the flipside of that I am glad that the process seemed to be drawn out. I was hurting in this process. I needed to heal rather than bleed fresh hurt onto the readers. It is possible to go through life doing things and not really operating in the purpose you were created for. You have to refuse to go back to a life of regret. Confront and acknowledge what is holding you back and stop living in the past.

Several years ago, this phrase used to come to my

mind, "The circumstances of life changes, when you change." At the time, I did not understand what it meant but deep down I knew it had some significance. This phrase plays a major part in my belief system. You have to come to a point in life where you understand that nothing changes until you make a choice to change. Change is a process. So do not let anyone tell you that change just happens. It does so after you make a conscious decision to engage in behavior that allows your life and circumstances to change.

POPULARIZING DRAMA
Chapter 13

I will be the first to admit that every day is not peaches and cream. Some days we may be all smiles and enjoyable to talk to, while on other days we may be moody or have a bad attitude. On our jobs, in our churches, in schools, or any other area of our lives we may encounter what is simply referred to as, "drama."

Drama has become so popular in American culture. Ironically, though many want to avoid the drama in their lives or eliminate it altogether. There are countless reality television shows, from secular families to Christian families that radiate drama. There seems to be a common pattern on those shows. The people are engaging in serious gossiping, backbiting, and fighting. While we are entangling ourselves so intently in their lives, we often forget that we have lives of our own. We have to remember that those people are being paid big bucks to highlight their issues on television. Sometimes, they are even playing a role and creating scenes just to gain the attention and draw viewers in. Reality shows can be addictive if you choose to let them be.

I was one of those drama queens so I can see why people are drawn to those types of shows. Remember, though, you have to guard what you expose your eyes and ears to. We have to be careful what we allow our spirits to experience. I no longer thrive on hearing the latest gossip or wonder what is going on in everyone else's business. I got to that point when I realized that my own drama consumed my life, so there was really no reason to add other drama to that mix.

I literally cringe when gossip or drama is taking place. I have to make an effort to avoid people who are extremely negative about situations or others. As God's children, we are to be Christ-like. When we interact with others on our jobs, they should be able to see Christ within us. It is not always easy, especially if you are dealing with difficult people. Jesus had to do the same. He is our example, so we should make an extra effort to represent Him at all times. When you are in Christ, you tend to view the world differently. We have to make sure that we are not causing the drama ourselves. If you truly listen to a gossiper, you will realize that the reason they are so wrapped up in others' lives is because they are trying to keep the focus off themselves. In other words, they may use gossip as a means to avoid their own pain or drama.

PROCRASTINATION
Chapter 14

I desperately wanted this book to be written and published, but I had to grapple with elements of fear. I had a pattern going on. I would write and stop and write and stop again. Fear would come in different ways and for different periods of time. The word, failure, played so much in my head that I could write a melody with that one word. I experienced different emotions in this process. I was excited and thought I could take on the world, while the next minute, I felt hopeless. I was definitely double-minded. How could I operate and even be successful in such a state of mind? I was waiting for approval of people who I thought should have been in my corner. Where was my cheerleading section?

> *Even if you're on the right track, you'll get run over if you just sit there.*
> Will Rogers

My fear was culminated with procrastination, which is something I have struggled with all of my life. Procrastination has caused me to miss out on opportunities. So, each time I sat at my computer ready to type, all kinds of thoughts would enter in my head. I also grappled with a fear of success. What if my book is received well? Will I still remain humble for the Lord? I would also get stuck on certain chapters and would pray for a breakthrough.

For many years, I knew what I wanted, or what I thought my purpose was, but did not have a clue how to operate in it. I went through so many cycles of helping others with their desires or purposes until I did not know how to help myself. Have you ever felt like that? You can help and push other people into the direction they need to go, but you have a hard time finding your

> *I don't wait for moods. You accomplish nothing if you do that. Your mind must know it has got to get down to work.*
>
> Pearl S. Buck

own direction. Really, there were others trying to push me too. I just used my favorite excuse, "I am going to do it." Ironically, things would either get done late or not at all. Sometimes, we can waste so much time professing what we want to do, but nothing ever gets completed. Accomplishments can only come when you take the time to do something.

I remember when I decided to go to college at the age of 33. I was not expected to even go to college. All of my life, I was told that I was a failure and would never make it. Even when I enrolled in college, my mother told me that I would never graduate and that it would rain and storm if I ever walked across a graduation stage. Of course that negativity made me fear more. I was so afraid of failing until I did everything at the last minute. I procrastinated on every work assignment, every test, and sometimes even going to class. I spent four years in college only to miss my June 2000 graduation with my colleagues. What happened? I procrastinated on finishing my final term paper that was due before graduation. Completing the paper was not the problem. I was more afraid of failing, and also afraid of the unknown. I did not know what was on the other side of the degree or what was expected of me once I completed it.

The unknown aspect of an experience can bring about real fear.

I had a friend at the time who told me the truth. She said, "If you are going to complete anything in your life, you have to finish this." The determination to complete something awoke in me, after she made that statement. I would go to her house and write, and she would stay up and help me finish my term paper. To make a long story short, I finished my paper and graduated from college in December 2000. My mother

> *Procrastination is the fear of success. People procrastinate because they are afraid of the success that they know will result if they move ahead now. Because success is heavy, carries a responsibility with it, it is much easier to procrastinate and live on the 'someday I'll' philosophy.*
>
> Dennis Waitley

was right, it did rain and storm on that day, but the sun literally came out as I walked across the stage. To God be the glory!

Could you be missing out on the purpose that God has called you to because of procrastination? Are you a talker or a doer? Do you make excuses of why something cannot be done? Do you talk yourself out of starting things? I wrote this chapter to see if there was anyone who could identify with my struggle. Once you recognize that you are holding yourself back then you will change.

This world is filled with corruption and immorality. We are to be beacons of light, shining and reflecting God's glory. There is so much we have to offer to the hurting people of this nation. Maybe there is a dream that you have put on the shelf. Do you desire to go back to school, start your own company, become a professional athlete, or even write a book? Seek the Lord and find what His will is for you. Stop procrastinating!

Here are a few tips I want to share with you: make a conscious decision to do something different; stop making excuses; and practice what you are afraid to do. So, if you are afraid to speak in public, practice in front of the mirror and change the way you talk to yourself. Say, I am or I will rather than I cannot. Be honest about the time you have to complete something. Make a schedule, set attainable goals, and go for it. Do not let weariness cause you to miss your assignment. Isn't it funny how staying awake when you have something important to do is always hard? Have you had that sleepy feeling when you know you needed to read the Bible or pray? Let your main thing be your main thing. Do not become so distracted with small things that you miss the bigger picture. Tackle what is important first. Sometimes, television or socializing with others can be distractions, so, learn to create a balance. Get out of the habit of waiting until tomorrow. Start today! Do not do anything based on your feelings. Sometimes your feelings can talk you right out of your blessings. Have you ever known that there was something you needed to do but you just did not feel happy about it? That is when you have to talk positive to yourself and remind yourself that you will not let your feelings or emotions dictate your life. Has anyone ever told you that you think too much? Sometimes, we can do just that. We can think ourselves right out of our assignments with, "what ifs?" What if this does not work? What if this is the wrong way? Better yet what if you never try? How would you know what worked or did not work?

So, when I say, "**it is not about you,**" it really is not. It is about the business of the Lord. If you see yourself in a procrastination cycle, please reexamine how you do things. Make a conscience effort to try something different. It took me eight years to finish writing this book. You know why it took that long? Procrastination! My last point to you is to remember that no matter what comes your way, you have the power to endure it. Just do it! Do not put it off or it may never get done.

LOOK WITHIN
Chapter 15

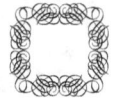

For many years I searched for love in all the wrong places. Whether it was through boyfriends, jobs, friends, or money, I continuously looked for love. Later on in life I realized that only God could give me the love I'd been searching for. Many people are walking around angry about life or with someone who hurt them. However, true love does not really come until you are complete within yourself.

I met a young lady named Heather. She often spoke of her loneliness and how she wished she was married. She just could not fathom why she was still single, while all of her friends were getting married. She desired to be married and out of the dating game. To others she used to pretend that she was content with being alone, but in private, she struggled with that fact. Being alone can be a bit scary, especially if you are not secure in who you are and you haven't figured out your purpose for being here on Earth.

As Heather and I talked, I shared a story with her about what I used to do when I was younger. I used to imagine myself having a boyfriend which would lead me to having the perfect family and living happily ever after. In the midst of those dreams, someone forgot to mention that I would experience the "in between" stuff that happened, like verbal and physical abuse, molestation, dishonesty, and cheating. I just had no idea that I would have to go through so much to reach my happily ever after.

Heather smiled and could identify with what I was saying. No one ever told me that love required me to work on my dysfunctional tendencies. I thought if I looked the part (referring to the outer appearance), things would be perfect in my world until my dying day. However, as I got older and wiser, I began to realize that life will always be filled with pleasant and unpleasant moments, no matter how good you think you are. Second Corinthians 4:17, "For our light affliction, which is but for a moment, worketh for us a far more exceeding and eternal weight of glory."

Let me tell you a little about Heather's story. Heather really dealt with a lot in her childhood. She constantly stayed in trouble at school and when her mom did show up at school, she was always intoxicated from the alcohol. She remembered all of those embarrassing moments. Many students who laughed at her as her mom staggered down the hallways. Her mom was also constantly strung out on drugs. Many members of her family drank daily. One night, as her family was sitting outside smoking, she heard sirens and saw blue lights coming down the street. At the time, she was nine and was not sure exactly what was going on. Her family was running from the porch only to realize that the sirens and the blue lights were coming to her house. She saw the police handcuff her mom and take her off to jail. It was at that moment, a feeling of hopelessness stirred in her heart. She acknowledged that her mom was not the best mom, but she was still her mom. Many of us have felt like that at one time or another. I told her that what I have come to realize is that a person can have the worst mom in the world, but underneath the layers of pain, anger, resentment, and unforgiveness, they still have love for their mom.

I have spoken with women in prison who are still hurting from what their mothers have done to them in their adolescence. Many of them were sold for drugs. Ironically, even though they are still angry, they long to hear their mothers say they're sorry. Heather admitted that she too is still waiting for her mom to apologize for the things that she let happen in her childhood. At age 10, she was taken away from her mom and placed in several foster homes. She could not talk to, or see her family. No one ever explained why she was placed in those foster homes. In five of those homes, she was either abused physically, verbally, or sexually. She never understood why no one came for her. What about the people who placed her there? Did they know she was being abused? Those were the questions she asked herself, as she spent the majority of her childhood with sorrow in her heart.

As time passed, she got older and was sent to live with her aunt. Her aunt took care of her, but there were other things going on in the small house of 13 that discouraged her. She constantly witnessed drinking, smoking, and fighting, so she began to believe that this was what life was all about. She began fighting at school and was taken to jail for beating up a girl. She stayed overnight at the Department of Juvenile Justice (DJJ). While she was at that facility, she thought it was the worst thing that could have ever happened. While she experienced many emotions, she was humiliated and scared at the same time. Even after the embarrassment and fright of that experience, she continued to do the same things once she left DJJ. She continued getting high, drinking, and having sex with any guy who uttered the word love. To this day, she said she is still trying to understand what true love really is.

Many people experience similar issues or circumstances. Often, people have no one to listen to or acknowledge their pain, or even notice that anything is wrong. This young lady longed for someone to care enough to listen. She wanted someone to help her find solutions or alternatives to help her be a better person, because what she was doing at the time was not working.

How many of you can admit that you were going through life, holding on to the hurt and pain from your childhood, yet hoping that things would get better? In fact, instead of the sunshine moments that we expect, things somehow seemed to get worse from day-to-day. As much as we say time heals all wounds, or we are just going to move on, some of us have gotten stuck in a routine of despair. We expect that one day it is will get better, but we do not really believe it will. So, doubt or lack of faith allows us to exist but not really function in life.

Heather never understood why she was repeating the same cycle. After listening to Heather's stories, I asked her if she wanted something different. I told her until she gets to a point where she is willing to do whatever it takes to move forward, she will stay stuck in whatever situation she is in, no matter how many people or things come along to help. Afterwards, she acknowledged that she did indeed want to do something different. Once she made that confession, the door was opened to offer her guidance, thus assisting her in her process of moving forward. John 16:33, says "These things I have spoken unto you, that in me ye might have peace. In the world ye shall have tribulation: but be of good cheer; I have overcome the world."

TAKING OFF THE MASK
Chapter 16

I am reminded of a story I once heard about a sparrow. Imagine a sparrow outside of a window of an office building that has an atrium full of beautiful, colorful plants, and trees of all shapes and sizes. The sparrow spots the magnificent garden, but does not notice the glass. Desiring to sit on a branch of one of those delightful trees, the sparrow flies toward the garden directly into the window. Visualize the stunned bird falling to the ground after impact. After a few minutes, you notice that the bird is no longer lying wounded on the ground. You look up only to see the poor, little sparrow propelling itself straight toward the window again at full speed. Inevitably, the bird slams into the window with a loud THUMP and tumbles to the ground. After a very short while, you observe the bird making a third attempt to fly through the window. The bird flies higher this time and goes into a spinning dive, but again, it hits the window. This goes on and on until the bird is injured.

The bird can be compared to an adult or adolescent.

> "What I am is good enough if I would only be it openly."
>
> *Carl Rogers*

We are constantly told what works and what does not, and we have that inward witness that guides us into all truth. However, we keep going through the same cycle; we keep running into that same window. I have noticed in my time as a counselor, and through my life experiences, that we walk around with many masks, pretending or trying to be something we are not. For years, I was hurt and damaged by the abuse I endured in my childhood and teen years. As a result, being around people was uncomfortable because I was always fearful of what people would think of me. On the outside, I looked happy. On the inside, I felt empty and alone. I was the mask-wearing queen until I dealt with my issues.

Am I alone in my masquerading? Certainly, I am not. It is amazing for me to see the large number of people wearing masks. I am astounded that the Lord has allowed me to encounter and minister to mask-wearers who are hanging on to past hurts. I say to you all, it is time to release the past, take off the masks, and be who God has called you to be.

I understand that taking off the mask will force you to deal with the real you. This can be scary if you do not know who you really are. What if the real you is somebody you could not face? I can say from experience, removing the masks that I wore for such a long time was an awakening moment. Not only was it an awakening experience, but also terrifying! I felt like I never knew myself at all. I had dislikes and interests that were hidden. I was very much the people pleaser. So, I kept my true desires hidden to everyone, including myself.

I met a young lady named Sheila. She participated in one of my workshops. It appeared that Sheila had it all together. She had a great job that afforded her the opportunity to hire someone to shop for her and her children. She lived in a nice home, in an upscale neighborhood. She owned two cars and an SUV. Sheila was also a pastor of a church. My husband and I decided to visit her church. Prior to service starting, we searched for her. Wow! In walked this beautiful, immaculately dressed lady from head-to- toe with a Bible and a briefcase. She was the ultimate professional, even at praising God. As time passed, I noticed something other than the beautiful exterior and outward persona. I noticed that Sheila was very unapproachable. I had a feeling that she was truly hurting and needed to be ministered to.

You see, it is becomes easier to spot hurting people, when you, in fact, have been hurting and have dealt with the scars of your youth. In turn, it's easier to recognize another fellow, mask-wearer. One thing God showed me through my process was that in order to effectively lead His people out of bondage, I had to be out of bondage. I had been ministering to God's people for a while, but was not able to effectively help them out of their bondage because I had not confronted the issues that had me bound. I refused to speak on certain topics, because they caused me great shame and pain.

One night after bible study, Sheila approached me and told me that God said I needed to finish my book. I will never forget that night. I went home in tears because she knew nothing about me writing a book and

I had been in a state of procrastination for a while. I knew that was God! I went home and picked up my book that I started several years ago and began writing again. This very same book that you are reading is the one I am speaking of. Glory be to God!

Sheila and I started talking on a consistent basis. The more we talked, the more I realized two things, Sheila was a hurting soul, and God was telling me she was my assignment. I had serious reservations regarding the second revelation. I thought, "No way, God, this woman has it together. How could I possibly help her?" Even in your unbelief, God can give you an assignment. You may wonder why He chose you, but, he will give you the grace to complete His tasks.

One Sunday afternoon after my husband and I were finishing up our dinner, I received a phone call. It was Sheila. It was so awesome to hear from her because I had been praying that God would open a door that would allow me to talk to her. During our brief phone conversation, she said God led her to call me to see if I would be willing to meet and talk with her. I was out of the house in less than 15 minutes. As I approached Sheila's house, I could not believe the neighborhood she lived in. The houses were really nice and really big. I truly had a wow moment in my head, when I pulled up to her house.

After we sat down on the couch, it appeared as if she was reluctant to talk. The conversation was a bit slow at first, but as time progressed, she began to ask questions. Not being certain if you can trust someone with what is really going on can be a big issue. Although Sheila was financially stable, she was no different from you or me. She was skeptical and a bit hesitant to talk about her life. I certainly understood because I was once like that. You want to share your story, but you are afraid that you will be judged.

In order to provide some sort of comfort for Sheila, I began talking about my life's issues. I told her what I endured in my childhood, adulthood, and about my failed suicide attempts. She was amazed that I could share my stories without any tears. Once I confronted those issues, I was no longer affected by the stigma or the realities of my stories. Sheila began to open up after that. She confessed that she was tired, felt drained, and was unsure of where she was going in life. As she spoke from the heart, her eyes began to fill with tears. She had a reputation of sophistication that she had to protect. She tried to hold back the tears. It was as if she refused to let them fall from her eyes.

I asked her if she was aware of the aura she was giving off at church. I told her that I believed she was a mighty woman of God, but perceived her to be an unapproachable one. I told her that after listening to her talk, while we sat on the couch, I thought God was trying to get her attention. I told her, in order for God to do what He needs to do, He needs to break her walls down and build her up to the woman He has called her to be. I went on to tell her that God will send many more people for her to minister to, but in order for her to be effective in their lives, she has to be relatable. I asked her if she could deal with the struggles of the people God would send her way. She began to tell me that her dad was not really there for her. She also talked about the pain she experienced after his death. She said her entire life revolved around her children and that her marriage was not in a good state. Finally, she let the tears fall from her eyes.

When she finished talking, she breathed a sigh of relief. It is amazing how much better you will feel once you confess your baggage. You will feel even more relieved once the baggage has been eliminated altogether. Believe me, it is a process. Was everything handled that day? Of course not, but we began to work the process. I told her I thought it would be beneficial for her to attend the classes, "Getting to the Root of the Problem," and "Making Peace with Your Past." She was a little reluctant about attending, but she finally agreed.

Attending the classes was a life-changing experience for her. She did not have a clue regarding who she was or how the past was currently affecting her present. Through the sessions, she realized that she had a shame-based identity and wore several masks. As you minister to people, it is important that you are willing to meet people where they are. If you are holding on to your stuff, it is hard to identify others' stuff. How so? Well, you are not going to allow them to get close enough to see the real you. I do not mean telling all of your business. What I mean is if you are ministering to someone who is going through what you have already conquered, be open and willing to share your story and tell them what brought you through. In other words, give some points, strategies, and scriptures. They need something that will give them tangible solutions to help them overcome their issues.

Sheila was a minister of the gospel, she owned her own company, and in her mind she thought she had it altogether. Just because you are in an authoritative position such as pastoring a church or counseling others, don't think you are exempt from experiencing issues. Many of you are possibly holding on to past childhood issues and are walking around with masks on. Your mask may be worn for several reasons, including fear, guilt, shame, unforgiveness, pain, or resentment. Yes, you can experience a feeling of discomfort when it is time to take those masks off. There may be times when you feel less authentic or even feel strange. You may think that if someone sees the real you, he or she will not like you.

If you are willing to get rid of your mask, I can help you. The process can be lengthy, but it will be well worth it. Being able to experience God's freedom and peace is an indescribable, liberating feeling. Isaiah 41:10, says, "Fear thou not; for I am with thee: be not dismayed; for I am thy God: I will strengthen thee; yea, I will help thee; yea, I will uphold thee with the right hand of my righteousness."

Here are three exercises you can do to start the process of taking off your mask: (1) Identify what mask you are wearing (examples, pain, fear, anger, etc.), (2) Decide which mask you want to get rid of and why, and (3) Confront each mask, one at a time.

DETERMINATION
Chapter 17

Just pray, it is going to be alright. Just keep pressing! God knows where you are. God is in control. Sounds familiar? I would always wonder where God was during all my mess. I'd say frequently say to myself, *"I am only a child. Why doesn't God protect me? If there is a God, why does He allow little children to be abused?"* I continually asked myself all of those questions as a little girl.

For years, I thought I was born with a curse. I questioned, *"Why is this not happening to any other family member? Why me? Why am I different?"* For many years, I thought I was the problem. From the time the abuse started until about the age of 33, my life seemed to be in turmoil. All I wanted as a little girl was to be loved and to be told that I was somebody. I grew tired of hearing that I was a mistake. I was about 33 years old when I finally confessed to someone what happened to me. James 5:16, says, "Confess your faults one to another, and pray one for another, that ye may be healed. The effectual fervent prayer of a righteous man availeth much."

I tried hard to prove to people who hurt me that I was not a bad child and I could make a difference. Even though it was hard growing up, I was still determined to be something other than what they were telling me I was. The words *stupid, dumb, unsuccessful, unattractive,* and *ignorant* constantly bombarded my mind. They were said so often but I did not have the strength to cast those negative words down.

I thought I was overcoming all of my obstacles by becoming numb to the pain. So, let us discuss what it means to be numb. It means you have no feeling or sensitivity in an area. I realize that there are many people who sit around numb to life's circumstances. Not feeling or pretending that I did not feel anything was a shield of protection. What I found out later during my process was that even though I was numb to my circumstances in the days of my youth, reality of the abuses I suffered resurfaced in my adult life. I was being fake with church folks. I was wearing an invisible mask, pretending to be something I was not. I used those techniques as coping mechanisms. Does any of this sound familiar to you? Can you relate at all to what I am saying?

After maturing in God's process, I began telling myself that no matter what comes my way I could handle it. As much as I thought God was not there, I realize now, He was the one who kept me from losing my mind throughout my childhood and into adulthood. Abuse was my experience. Even if you were not physically, verbally, or sexually abused, perhaps there was something in your background that caused you to pick up this book. Is there something in your past that has prevented you from moving forward in the purpose God has predestined for you?

I had to confront the unforgiveness and resentment I had in my heart for many years, I had to face the giants that tore me down. How can one do that? My answer to you is--one step at a time. What is your giant? What is it that has kept you from experiencing freedom?

Pure determination is the key. No matter what people thought about me or what I was told growing up, I started believing in myself. If you have done things in the past to cause pain, or someone has caused you pain, make peace with it and move forward. There are people who will try to hold you in a self-defeating pattern, but you have to be determined not to allow that to happen.

Luke 1:37, says, "For with God nothing shall be impossible." I quoted that scripture daily to give me hope. It is my suggestion that you also grab hold of something positive and do not let go. I have some suggestions for you that can help you renew your minds. If you are constantly in the presence of negative people it is necessary for you to change who you are hanging around. Reading self-help books can help shed light on your situation. Also, you must keep your mind stayed on Jesus. In your car, listen to worship music or motivational messages that inspire you.

LET GO AND LET GOD
Chapter 18

In September 2012, my son came from Vancouver, Washington to live with me. There was a change in his flight once he reached Detroit, Michigan, and he was expected to be in Charlotte, North Carolina, around 9:45 p.m. My husband and I left home, heading to Charlotte to meet him. On the way to the airport, we received a call from my sister saying that my son missed his flight. He did not even call to tell me what happened. Once I got in touch with him, sadness arose in my spirit as I learned that he intentionally missed his flight. I should have known that something was not quite right when I spoke to him earlier. He said if he could not get another flight he would be stuck in Detroit. He even suggested that he just stay in Detroit for the night and get a room. I was not in agreement with that plan, and suggested that he stay in the airport and get on the next flight. My son just wanted to check out Detroit, because he always wanted to go there. At the time, I did not know that.

My sister picked him up from the airport on Saturday morning in Charlotte and brought him to Columbia, South Carolina. She complained about how he smelled and that he desperately needed a haircut. I was a bit shocked because before he left Vancouver, Washington, I asked his father to make sure he got a haircut. I later found out that my son refused to cut his hair, even at his father's request. I told my sister to meet me at the barber shop. I asked no questions because I was the parent. I asked the barber to cut all of his hair off.

My son and I had an interesting conversation. I found out that he spent some time on the streets in a homeless situation. He said he had people talking to him in his head and that he knew others' thoughts. He declared that he was immortal and had been shot in the head. For the first couple of days, we engaged in those types of strange conversations. Not long after he came to S.C., he was ready to go back. He said I was holding his life up and that he wanted to go back to Vancouver. He admitted he could not get a job because he could not pass the drug tests.

My husband typed up a contract for my son to sign while he stayed with us. The contract stated all the rules we expected him to abide by. When asked to sign, my son just drew a line as if that was his signature. Of course, that was unacceptable. He refused to sign his entire name. He called us crazy. At that moment, my husband asked him to leave. As much as I loved my son, I was in agreement with my husband. We reiterated that we were only trying to help him. We reminded him that we were taking care of him. He had food to eat, clothes to wear, and a place to lay his head, but he was very unappreciative. So, he got his book bag and got in the car. I told him that all he needed to do was apologize and do something different. He still was not in agreement, so we drove him downtown convinced that he will learn one way or the other. I took his cell phone and told him to get out of the car. Since he had all the answers and wanted things his way, he needed to figure out how he was going to get back to Vancouver. We told him that we loved him and would continue to pray for him. My heart was broken and I cried as we left him. I was just astonished at how abnormal my son was acting.

Around 1:45 a.m. Tuesday morning, I received a call from an unidentified number. I thought it was my mom calling with an update on my dad's condition, because he had been really sick. However, it was actually my son on the line, asking me to come and get him. I told him that he needed to talk to my husband. After that brief conversation, we went to pick him up from the bus station. Before he could get into the car, he knew he had to apologize. He did and seemed happy to be home in a bed again.

Rules are rules. We asked him not to play or record negative music in the house or post anymore negative messages on Facebook and Twitter. Proverbs 18:21, says, "Death and life are in the power of the tongue: and they that love it shall eat the fruit thereof." Clearly, we must watch what we say and that also includes typing. We were trying to protect him from dwelling in negativity. He insisted on doing things his way. For example, he started posting from my mom's computer while he visited her home. Proverbs 19:21, says, "There are many devices in a man's heart; nevertheless the counsel of the Lord, that shall stand."

I did not know what to do anymore. I thought, "How can I possibly reach my son?" All night long, I tossed and turned. On Saturday morning, I woke up and my husband informed me that he was taking my son to a men's prayer breakfast. That gave me some time to pray and spend time with God. I thought about God's awesomeness and I was appreciative of where he had brought me from. I asked, "Lord, what am I going to do with my son? I want only to protect him."

I was definitely happy about them heading to prayer together. I got dressed and was on my way to meet a friend at the library. I forgot something and had to go back upstairs. As I was about to leave, I barely stepped outside my house and heard my husband telling me to call the police. My son's eye was bleeding. I screamed and asked what was going on. We had already asked my son not to smoke cigarettes in the house or in our yard. On this morning, he chose to do so anyway. My husband reminded him about our no cigarette rule and my son brushed up against him and began mouthing off. He grabbed my son and physical exchanges started. My son punched him in the eye, followed by my husband punching him in the face. Truly, this was the worst day of my life. It is ironic that just when you think things can't get any worse, they do. My husband ended up calling the police. I was too distraught to make that call, and I was a bit scared. I called my friend instead and told her that I could not make the library trip. She heard the discomfort and distress in my voice and told me she was on her way.

After the police arrived, they spoke with my husband and son. While they were talking, I just had this overwhelming feeling that it was really time for my son to leave. There was a bus leaving at 1:45 p.m., and I knew my son had to be on it. I did not have a clue about how I would get the money for the ticket. I had only a portion of the money, but my decision was made. I even thought of using the money I had for my multiple sclerosis medication toward the ticket. I prayed to God. I asked, "If this is your will Lord, let this be done." Suddenly, I received a call from my sister. I told her what was going on, and she agreed to help me with the ticket. At 1:45 p.m., my son was on the bus heading to Vancouver.

Some of you might wonder how a mother could make such a decision. As a parent, we sometimes have to make hard decisions. It may seem like cruel and unusual punishment at first, but in the long run we pray that the lessons will be learned and mistakes will not be repeated. Proverbs 22:6, says, "Train up a child in the way he should go: and when he is old, he will not depart from it." My son had a one track mind and that was to do things his way and on his terms. In the end, I knew that I had to turn him over to the Lord. I had to believe and I did believe that the God I serve will work this situation out for all of our good. Wow, I had to let go and let God. I am not going to pretend that it was a good feeling. It was hurtful and caused pain, but it had to be done.

For you, my dear readers, get on your knees and tell God that He is bigger than any of the situations that you may be dealing with right now. Let go and let God! Making the decision to give up control and allow God to be God is not always easy. However, it must be done. Otherwise, we will continue to be burdened by the circumstances of life.

My son is going through his process right now. So, I know that he will be fine. Proverbs 3:5-6, says, "Trust in the Lord with all thine heart; and lean not unto thine own understanding. In all thy ways acknowledge him, and he shall direct thy paths." Whatever you may be going through right now, know that God knows where you are. Hebrews 13:5, says, "Let your conversation be without covetousness; and be content with such things as ye have: for he hath said, I will never leave thee, nor forsake thee." God loves you!

CHANGE (PART 1)
Chapter 19

In today's society, many people are searching for, or looking for a change. When Barack Obama won the presidential election, he spoke from the subject of change. What kind of change are you looking for? Are you looking for change in your home, change at work, change in your relationships, or even change in yourself? Change is a word that can incite a multitude of feelings. It can be feelings of excitement or of disappointment. Change can be exciting, because it can indicate a desire for something new; a fresh beginning. However, fear can arise with the mere utter of the word. For example, change indicates that there is a disparity in who you are, versus how God or others view you. Are there elements of your character that can benefit from change? Can you become a better person through change? That is what you have to ask yourself.

What I came to realize is that just because people say they want to change, does not mean they are willing to do what it takes to make the change. It is so disturbing

> *"You are the way you are because that's the way you want to be. If you really wanted to be any different, you would be in the process of changing right now."*
> Fred Smith

to sit and talk to people who want and need change but are afraid of change. They are afraid to get out of their comfort zones. Transitions can be a bit frightening, especially when you do not know what the outcome will be. I see an image of a turtle. The turtle sticks its head out of the shell, and when something comes along, it quickly hides its head. Many people are the same way. They want to get better and do something different, but when something comes along and sidetracks them, they run back into their shells.

Let us talk for a moment about alterations. When it was time to make changes in my life, I did not feel I needed to alter anything. I just wanted something different. I used the same saying that many people who don't want to get out of their comfort zones use, "Nothing is wrong with me. I am good." That was so far from the truth. I was a total mess and I thought if I changed anything, everything would just fall apart. I kept asking the Lord to help me. I was jealous because I saw Him helping everybody else. Little by little, I began to realize that everybody else wanted to be helped by God. I said I did, but did I really? I thought as long as you go to the altar and repent it was okay to do whatever you want. That sure was the wrong mindset. I learned that when you repent, you must change your ways, otherwise you are just uttering words. That is why your heart will not change, until you are truthful about your need for change. I am all for independence and I think being a unique individual is great. However, confessing that people must accept you as you are is not always a good statement. Who you are may not be who God desires

> "The circumstances of life change when you change."
>
> *Valerie Hodge Lane*

you to become. He wants you holy. He wants you in His perfect will. Jeremiah 1:5, says, "Before I formed thee in the belly I knew thee; and before thou camest forth out of the womb I sanctified thee, and I ordained thee a prophet unto the nations."

Let me tell you about Charlene. She was such an angry person, although she participated weekly in our, "Making Peace with Your Past," group. On her first day, she stressed that she came to the class because she heard about the support group and needed a change. She was unsure of what that change actually was at the time, and she later confessed that she did not know why she was there. I asked her if she wanted to change. On many occasions I wanted to change, mainly because I was told that I needed it. However, change was not going to happen until I decided that I was ready for it. I stressed to Charlene that when she really gets tired, she will be more willing to do whatever it takes to make a change.

As she sat in the group and listened for a couple of weeks, she identified with others in the group. Her story went back to her parents divorcing when she was 12. The discord in her family caused her to take on the role as the perfect child. She thought if she would do more or make better grades, then her parents would somehow get back together. She blamed herself, but of course, it was not her fault. She spent a majority of her adult life trying to please people just to be accepted. During our sessions, she began to examine the reasons behind her decision to go to college. She wanted to become a doctor. She thought that an occupation of that nature would surely gain acceptance from her parents.

Charlene held on to so much, until she became numb. She was hurting from events of her childhood. That is why so many hurting people are hurting other people. Change is not just a saying, it is an action. Even though Charlene was hard to talk to at the beginning, she began releasing all she was feeling. It was years of hurt that came through in her tears. It was at this point she desired to change and to take the necessary steps to make the change. Through her process, she became a totally different person. This process did not happen overnight. Slowly, she changed how she interacted with people, and she changed how she thought about herself. She finally realized that she had purpose and that her life was not a waste.

CHANGE (PART 2)
Chapter 20

Philippians 3:12, says, "Not as though I had already attained, either were already perfect: but I follow after, if that I may apprehend that for which also I am apprehended of Christ Jesus." I am not going to sit here and tell you that changing will be a cake walk. That is not always the case, in fact, it can be hard. If changing was easy, there would not be so many out there holding on to their past hurts. Take a moment to think. Is there something or someone that has been holding you back from moving forward? Your answer actually may be that you are okay with who you are. That is fine. I thank God that you have it together. However, for those who are not satisfied with who you are and do not know how to go about changing, just know that I too, was so fed up with failing at every angle in my life and I gave up many times.

I felt totally hopeless, and the only thing that kept me sane was attending church. I did, however, experience loneliness there, as well, because everyone else seemed to have it together. I am just saying that change was hard. I wanted to change, but I just didn't know how to change. The people around me would tell me that I would be okay if I just prayed. That used to bother me so much. For goodness sake, I was praying. I just did not believe that God was listening to me. People need direction and a sense of hope. Just telling someone to pray does not always cut it. Yes, prayer is necessary, but you also have to allow God to use you so you can help guide others out of their situations.

"Making Peace with Your Past," is the support group that helped me overcome my issues, and it's ironic that now I minister through that same group, helping others overcome. Here is how I first got involved with the group. One day while sitting at a friend's house, she saw a newspaper ad for a class that she thought would be beneficial for me. At first, I was sort of reluctant about going, but I was tired of repeating the same cycle. At this point, I was willing to do whatever it took to make a change. Notice, I said I did something. I took action. Even though it was very scary, I needed a change, so I went to my first, "Making Peace with Your Past," class.

You have to make a decision to move forward. I talk about getting to the root of the problem because many people self-medicate and pray things will just go away. Others just go along in life pretending they are alright. Life and situations do not always turn out the way we want. We can suppress our true feelings, only to find out later on in life, they have a way of seeping out. Do not be afraid to step out and make a change. Change not only helps you, but also causes you to help others.

Do not let people discourage you from sharing your stories with others. Those are your testimonies. Your testimony is not just for you, it is to help others, as well. Care less what others may think of you as you share gruesome details of your past. You never know how many people will be delivered, as a result of your testimony. In other words, whatever you have gone through or have been delivered from, can actually save someone else's life. Many churches are hurting because there are people in leadership roles who have not been delivered from their own issues. Therefore, they are only able to minister out of their emotions and not from the anointing of God.

How bad do you want change? Regardless of what is

going on in your life at this moment, you can change. My question to you is do you really want change? Regardless of your past or your present, make a commitment to do something different.

Even writing this book took commitment. I had to fight my own thoughts as well as the naysayers who said it would never happen. It may have taken years, but look at God! I am here sharing these stories with you. Determination is the key to unlocking the doors to changing your circumstances. Think of the effect you could have on the world if you are willing to let God work the kinks out in your life.

I definitely can say that writing this book has motivated me to reach my full potential as a daughter of God, as a wife, as a friend, as a mother, and as a speaker. Regardless of what has occurred in our lives, we must make changes. Sure, we can justifiably argue that we have a right to be negative or destructive because of abuse, neglect, or poverty in our childhood. However, we have to acknowledge that our state of mind can often hold us back. We have to realize that the people in our lives may have failed us, but that does not define who we are. In other words, yesterday is gone, and today is a new day. Do you believe that changing our present actions can have a positive result on our future outcomes? Second Peter 1:5-8, says, "And beside this, giving all diligence, adds to your faith virtue; and to virtue knowledge; and to knowledge temperance; and to temperance patience; and to patience godliness; and to godliness brotherly kindness; and to brotherly kindness charity. For if these things be in you, and abound, they make you that ye shall neither be barren nor unfruitful in the knowledge of our Lord Jesus Christ."

DO NOT QUIT
Chapter 21

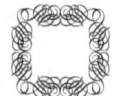

I wanted to give up on life many times. I was depressed, lonely, insecure, sad, and confused for the majority of my life. The sad part is, no one really noticed. I spent many years trying to please a mother who refused to validate that I was even important or even offer me unconditional love. I looked for love in all the wrong places, throughout my adolescence and part of my adulthood. After being miserable for so many years, I made matters worse by playing the blame game. I thought, "If my mother would just have loved me, I would not have ended up like this. I am this way because of everyone else." Yes, I was victimized for several years of my life and have been in pain on a consistent basis. Ultimately, I had to learn that taking Tylenol PM every night was not helping. My pain was much deeper than I realized. Have you ever felt that way? Have you ever felt that the pain was so deep that you would not be able to make it to the next day? Did you even care if the next day would come or not? Did you ever just want to give up on life altogether? I know I certainly have and it is not a good feeling.

We have to figure out what is causing the anger and bitterness in our hearts. It is so easy to say we will get over it and move on, or even listen to others telling us to do the same. Ultimately, we must not quit. God has something better in store for each of us.

UNDERSTANDING PURPOSE THROUGH YOUR PAIN
Chapter 22

As I began writing this book, I became stuck in my thoughts on numerous occasions and unable to write without tears streaming down my face. Remembering the pain and confusion of my life and rehashing them was a bit overwhelming at times. However, that is expected to happen, and you will experience those feelings when your process of healing begins. Simply purging my heart so that others may benefit kept me going. That was done to convey my simple message that it's not about us. With each emotion and with each story that I wrote, I had to focus on you, my dear brothers and sisters. I came to realize that I had to learn to write from my heart, instead of my emotions. Writing from emotions speaks at people. Writing from the heart speaks to people.

As you have read in earlier chapters, my life was more than a challenge, and yet I am still here. I have come to acknowledge that God had me in a waiting pattern. Waiting can seem so long at times. For some of us who desire true deliverance, there is no other option but to wait. What was I waiting for? I was waiting for God to do His handiwork.

All of the pain, rejection, disappointments, anger, and bitterness were a part of the process to push me into my purpose. I would never deny or minimize what

I have gone through or even what you have gone through. Pain hurts and to believe otherwise is unwise. Psalm 18:49, says, "Therefore will I give thanks unto thee, O Lord, among the heathen, and sing praises unto thy name." No, it did not always feel good while I was going through, but I am thankful for making it to the other side. That other side consists of joy and peace forever more. All of your problems may not go away instantly, but you can rest in the comfort of knowing that God is there with you.

Let me take a moment to thank God.

"Dear God, these things, circumstances, and events did not kill me. Although at times, I felt as if they would. You used them to make me stronger, Lord. Yes, I wanted to die. Yes, I wanted to give up. Yes, Father, there were many times that I was upset with You for not coming to help me. I know that you were indeed doing just that. Harvest takes time. Because of You, I truly understand humility and what it is really like to depend on You. Most importantly Father, You taught me how to worship You in spirit and in truth. Wow! I did not know that the most important relationship that came out of this madness of my life was the one we have created together. Having a relationship with You, keeps me encouraged, even in discouraging moments."

No matter where you are right now, understand that this too shall pass. When I felt like throwing in the towel, there was always this still, small voice echoing the following words, "You are stronger than you think you are." I did not understand how those words could even apply to me. I do not mean to sound cliché'ish, but when I look back over my life, I realize that my steps were really being ordered by the Lord. I never experienced that knowledge until I took the focus off me and started helping others. It was then, when I noticed that my life was starting to move in an entirely different direction. Instead of letting my circumstances continue to dictate me, I started dictating my circumstances. You have the power to initiate change in your life, regardless of what is happening or what has happened in your life.

A CALL TO SALVATION
Chapter 23

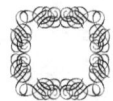

This is a sinful world. We have to learn to be in it and not of it. God desires for all of us to be reunited with Him. If you have not accepted Jesus Christ into your life or you want to rededicate your life to Christ, here is your chance to do so.

Confess your sins to the Lord and repeat after me: "I believe that Jesus Christ died on the cross. He did that as a penalty for my sins. I invite Jesus into my life. I want to be saved." Second Corinthians 5:17, says "Therefore if any man be in Christ, he is a new creature: old things are passed away; behold, all things are become new."

My readers, you have now entered the kingdom of God as a born-again believer.

CONCLUSION

As I move forward, I can say my life has been a dream come true. It's not perfect but it is wonderful. My dad died in 2012 from Chronic Obstructive Pulmonary Disease (COPD). Before he died I had to make peace with my past. For me to move forward I had to forgive him. Crazy sounding, huh? Why would I need to do something like that? First, God says, "Vengeance is mine." He also gave me what I needed so I could forgive, and I want to share it with you.

First, I had to recognize that I grew up in a dysfunctional family. My family believed that what happened in the house, stayed in the house. I remember them saying "Girl you better not go out there talking about our business. What goes on in this house, stays in this house!" That taught me not to talk about what I was going through. It's funny how it's so easy to keep your troubles all bottled up inside, but truth be told, you must talk about it. You must let it out. Keeping it inside is what keeps you hurting. Don't keep your troubles bottled up. Bottling up your issues causes stress. It causes you to be mad and not even know why or that you are even mad. For example, a friend could be all smiles and joyful one day, then another day they don't even want to speak. You probably thought that friend was just being nasty, but no, what's probably going on is he or she has been stuffing feelings somewhere down in the unconscious mind or buried low in the soul; then suddenly without warning, it's leaks out in the way that express themselves around people. I call it the Soda effect; when you shake up the bottle and loosen the top just a little, some of the soda will erupt out. If you ease the pressure slowly at first, it will seep out a little, but if you are unaware of the pressure of the shook can, it could have a violent conclusion. You will be caught up in its devastating affects; soda gone bad all over you.

You must get to a point; I know it's not easy, where you start talking about your problems. It's not easy because most people find it hard to trust. Some think, why should I tell someone my business just so they can go and tell everyone else? Don't let it trouble you, it's your trash. If you take out the trash and someone picks it up, it's just trash. I need you to recognize that if you take out trash at home, you don't care what name of the person who picks it up; all you know is Sanitation is picking it up.

Next, start surrounding yourself with people who are going in a positive direction and are doing positive things. Attend one of the local professional speaking bureaus, they always have wonderful speakers who are talking about positive things and you will meet positive people. Step out of your box!

As for me, I'm allergic to negativity now. I had to change my mindset from being one who complained about what wasn't going right with me seeing all the things that are going right. So, get those negative thoughts out of your head! Find what is going good in your life! It doesn't have to be something big find just that one little thing to focus on.

Third, express your feelings. Expressing your feelings is not supposed to be hard; it's supposed to be easy. You may not know how to start expressing your feelings, so as a help, start by looking in your mirror and telling yourself you're beautiful, and that you're worthy. Finally, tell yourself that you deserve of all the goodness that God has to give you. Grab a sticky note or some paper and tape positive notes where you can see them every day and repeat them to yourself. There's a song that says, "Encourage Yourself." The sticky notes represent your reinforcement or your encouragement. By doing this, you will begin the path of taking control back in your life.

I know it seems like such a simple approach, but watch it work wonders. Okay, now that you are speaking positive things, you must start believing. This is no Freudian complicated answer you might have been expecting. the thing is, the lessons that God gives us are not complicated, that way everyone can do it.

Practicing these steps brought me to a point where I was able to go to my father and forgive him. I have told my father that I love him. I hugged him, but I did this for him, I did it for me. It allowed me to move forward and take control of what God has in store for me. You won't believe how much of a release that was for me. If you still find it hard to forgive someone who hurt you, remember this "hurting people HURT other people." That person who hurt you probably was probably hurt at some point in his life. If you're going to be loving and whole, you'll have to work what I have been telling you and watch it change your life.

My Mother and I talk on a daily basis now. I told her how she made me feel as a child. I let her know how I believed she wasn't protecting me. After we finally had this conversation, I found out she did not know what was going on, and she actually thought she was doing a great job as a mother. Since then, she apologized for not being there for me, but before she even apologized, I had already forgiven her. Forgiveness is not for the other person it's for you. She's retired Now and enjoying life with her boyfriend who treats me like a daughter.

Now getting back with my mom wasn't all gravy. When we would talk by phone, there were times I had to put the phone on mute because I had to stay away from her negativity. Don't get me wrong my mom is a good woman but she was raised in a time where people could not see what God really had in store for them. Therefore, she spoke about what she couldn't see and what wasn't being done. Well, I see the world for what it is; a world for me to enjoy and to live to the fullest.

It has always been a dream for me to write my story and help heal the broken hearted. Oh, by the way, my dream now is to meet Oprah Winfrey, T.D. Jakes, Les Brown, and Tyler Perry. I haven't met yet, but I believe it's going to happen.

After all my hurt and pain, I am here to tell you that no matter what you're going through, God can bring you through. If He can do it for me, I guarantee He'll do it for you.

What I need to warn you about is that this is just the beginning. There will be other obstacles that will come your way. Never fear, if you stay on your course you will make it through. I just know, "It's Not About Me, I understand there is purpose through my pain!"

ACKNOWLEDGEMENTS

Thank you, Heavenly Father, for trusting me to share with Your people. God, You deserve all of the honor and glory. You continue to order my steps and keep me even when I don't want to be kept. You are an awesome God! Jeremiah 29:11, says, "For I know the thoughts that I think toward you, saith the Lord, thoughts of peace, and not of evil, to give you an expected end." I thank you, Jesus, for interceding on my behalf. Thank you, Holy Spirit, for comforting me through this healing process.

Darryl, my husband, I thank you for always keeping me on track. Daily, you would come home and inquire about what I have written. You are truly a wonderful husband and I am thankful that God brought us together. I thank you for your patience and encouragement. I love you very much! The best is yet to come for both of us!

Deron, you are truly my inspiration. I thank God that I have you as my son. You prayed when I was too weak to pray for myself. Thank you, sunshine!

Mommy and Daddy, I thank God for the relationship that we have now. I will not deny that it was rough growing up. God is a God of restoration. He has restored our relationship and I am thankful for your love. I love you both very much!

Debra, you are an amazing woman of God. I

appreciate you and am so proud to have you as my little sister. Thank you for all that you do! I love you!

I can say that I have some terrific friends. Veronica, Ray, Kathryn, Terri, Yakesha, Victoria, and Katisha, you all are simply the best! I thank you all for believing in me, despite the naysayers. You kept encouraging me to walk by faith and not by sight. I did not give up, and I thank you for your prayers.

Thanks to my wonderful in-laws, Epifania, Gale, Stacey, Tameka, Shakeem, Elliott, and Cybil, whom I love very much.

Pastor Darrell Jackson, Pastor Karlton Dixon, and First Lady Lisa Dixon, thank you for serving as my spiritual leaders. God has used you to open my eyes to His goodness. Thank you for showing me how to walk as a woman of God, according to His Holy Word.

Finally, I want to thank you, Lisa. You are truly a Godsend. You are such an awesome woman of God. Thank you for being obedient to the voice of God to me. Thank you for believing in the God in me, and helping me to bring this book to fruition. You are a true blessing. First Corinthians, 15:58, says, "Therefore, my beloved brethren, be ye steadfast, unmovable, always abounding in the work of the Lord, forasmuch as ye know that your labour is not in vain in the Lord."

BIBLE REFERENCES

All Bible verses are from the King James Version (KJV) Bible.

Acknowledgements
    Jeremiah 29:11

Chapter 1: It's Not About You
Genesis 50:20
Psalm 139:8
Isaiah 26:3
Psalm 1:2
Romans 8:1
John 10:10

Chapter 2: Getting Pass Your Past
James 4:17

Chapter 3: A Decade of Abuse
Mark 4:15

Chapter 4: Tore Up from the Floor Up (Part 1)
James 4:4
Deuteronomy 30:19

Chapter 5: Tore Up from the Floor Up (Part 2)
Philippians 3:14

Chapter 6: Identity Thief
Philippians 4:13
Romans 8:37
Psalm 77:2
Philippians 4:8

Chapter 7: Dysfunctional Families (Part 1)
Luke 1:37

Chapter 8: Dysfunctional Families (Part 2)
Romans 8:1

Chapter 9: The Hedge of Protection
Matthew 6:33

Chapter 10: Getting to the Root of the Problem
2 Corinthians 10:5

Chapter 11: Forever the Victim
Genesis 50:20

Chapter 15: Look Within
2 Corinthians 4:17
John 16:33

Chapter 16: Taking Off the Mask
Isaiah 41:10

Chapter 17: Determination
James 5:16
Luke 1:37

Chapter 18: Let Go and Let God
Proverbs 18:21
Proverbs 19:21
Proverbs 22:6
Hebrews 13:5

Chapter 19: Change (Part 1)
Jeremiah 1:5

Chapter 20: Change (Part 2)
Philippians 3:12
2 Peter 1:5-8

Chapter 22: Understanding Purpose Through Your Pain
Psalm 18:49

Chapter 23: A Call to Salvation
2 Corinthians 5:17

INSPIRATIONAL QUOTES

Chapter 5: Tore Up from the Floor Up

When obstacles arise, you change your direction to reach your goal; you do not change your decision to get there. – Zig Ziglar

Source: http://www.goodreads.com

Chapter 14: Procrastination

I don't wait for moods. You accomplish nothing if you do that. Your mind must know it has got to get down to work. – Pearl S. Buck

Source: http://www.brainyquote.com

Even if you're on the right track, you'll get run over if you just sit there. – Will Rogers

Source: http://www.brainyquote.com

Procrastination is the fear of success. People procrastinate because they are afraid of the success that they know will result if they move ahead now. Because success is heavy, carries a responsibility with it, it is much easier to procrastinate and live on the 'someday I'll' philosophy. – Dennis Waitley

Source: http://quotationsbook.com

Chapter 16: Taking off the Mask

What I am is good enough if I would only be it openly. – Carl Rogers

Source: http://excellentquotations.com

ABOUT THE AUTHOR

Valerie Hodge Lane, 1965, South Carolina born, has a Bachelor's of Science degree in Business Administration  and a Master's of Science degree in Human Services. She is an accomplished and sought-after inspirational speaker, entrepreneur, and domestic violence advocate. Her goal is to, "Get to the Root of the Problem," and to inspire others to move pass their past and progress into a world of hope, triumph, and accomplishment. She has spoken to thousands of people from all walks of life on topics that range from personal and professional growth, to the development of healthy relationships and love.

Over the years, Valerie has taken on a multitude of roles because of the challenges that have come into her life. While she was conquering those obstacles, she realized that she must share with the world, the tools she was given. She has lectured on the collegiate level, as well as conducted open forums for men, women, and teenagers. She has facilitated individual and group counseling sessions, most notably, "Making Peace with Your Past," therapeutic support groups. Valerie served as a vice-president of Mothers Against Drunk Driving. She was co-chairperson of the Lee County Domestic Violence Coalition of South Carolina and also served on the Board of the Lee County Center Teen Advisory Board. She has developed and implemented workshops for A Better Way: Project GO "Gang Out." She has also worked as a victim's advocate for Sistercare, Inc. of South Carolina.

Valerie has spoken in front of large audiences, such as the National Organization for Victim Assistance (NOVA) National Conference, Without Walls International Church (under the direction of Paula White), and as a keynote speaker at the National Mean Girls Conference. She has presented to smaller audiences, such as the South Carolina School Counselors Association and The Department of Juvenile Justice Management Team.

Valerie is married to Darryl Lane and has a son named Deron Sample, Jr. She is the founder and President of Positive Image Consulting Firm.

ABOUT THE POSITIVE IMAGE CONSULTING FIRM

Valerie H. Lane is the founder of the Positive Image Consulting Firm. God took the traumatic situations of her life, cleaned her up from the inside out, and blessed her to operate a business that helps to reshape the mindset of hurting people and those in need of transformation. Being no respecter of persons, she is blessed to work with various types of people in different age groups, as well as different genders. She believes there is no greater experience than to be blessed by God and to bless others.

Positive Image Consulting Firm is a faith-based organization that assists hurting people during their healing processes. The organization offers vital information needed to start the healing cycle, and programs geared toward a better quality of life approach. These programs are intended to benefit the individuals and inspire them to keep pressing forward.

It is a goal that the Positive Image Consulting Firm brand will expand to the media to help the healing cycle from a spiritual angle. In addition to helping adults, it is also an objective to address the challenges and offer coping skills to our youth.

The Positive Image Consulting Firm cannot exist without the collective efforts of Valerie Lane, Darryl Lane (husband), Deron Sample, Jr. (son), and her co-workers and friends -- Yakesha Means, Billy Shiver, and Elizabeth Shirley Lloyd. This organization would not function properly without these workers. They understand purpose, hard work, the power of prayer, and the omnipotence of God.

Positive Image Consulting Firm offers the following inspirational workshops:

(1) Stop Looking Back and Move Forward
(2) Going through the Process
(3) Change Begins with You
(4) You Have What it Takes
(5) Follow Your Dreams
(6) You are the Conqueror
(7) Making Peace with Your Past
(8) Getting to the Root of the Problem

Valerie and her staff will be offering the following workshops in the future:

(1) Freedom Café
(2) What about the Parents?
(3) Men of Vision
(4) Out of the Ashes College Survival Series
(5) Teens are People too

For more information on the Positive Image Consulting Firm, please visit our website at:

www.positiveimageconsulting.org
vlane@positiveimageconsulting.org

www.ingramcontent.com/pod-product-compliance
Lightning Source LLC
Chambersburg PA
CBHW051952290426
44110CB00015B/2215